The Kitchen Design Company's
Kitchen Design Idea Book

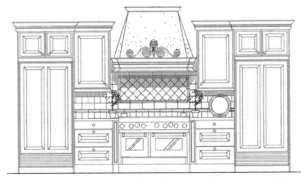

Copyright © 1997-2015 The Kitchen Design Company - All rights reserved

50 Different Custom Kitchens - 50 Different Plans & Perspective Drawing Sets
Makes Designing Your New Kitchen Easy!

Joe Brandao

Copyright © 2015 The Kitchen Design Company
All rights reserved.
ISBN: 1522752684
ISBN-13: 978-1522752684

All rights reserved. No part of the contents of these drawings may be reproduced or transmitted in any form or by any means without the written permission of the publisher.

Kitchen Design Company books are available on our webstore.
Visit our webstore at www.KitchenDesignCompanyStore.com
Visit our website at www.KitchenDesignCo.com
Send comments to: **ask@KitchenDesignIdeaBook.com**

DISCLAIMER

The Kitchen Design Company (TKDC) is providing these drawings consisting of the cabinetry plans, and 3D perspective drawings for design purposes only. They are to be used only as a guide, because they are schematic design drawings not intended to be used for construction under any circumstances.

These drawings are to be used as a guide to express the home owners design intent and TKDC accepts no responsibility for their accuracy, use, or misuse. No warranty is made with respect to the accuracy or completeness of the information shown or referenced in these drawings. TKDC specifically disclaims and responsibility for any liability, loss or risk, personal or otherwise, which is incurred as a consequence, directly or indirectly, of the use and application of any of the contents of this book.

We strongly suggest you engage the assistance of local design professionals and trades people familiar with this type of construction project. All of our projects have been created with the assistance of qualified architects, designers, electricians, plumbers, and most importantly, general contractors all familiar with local building codes, and processes required to tackle this type of extensive construction.

Kitchen Design Idea Book

Table Of Contents

Plan	Page
97001	1
97030	3
0028	5
97020	7
98062	9
0027	12
97006	16
98060	19
98074	21
98003	23
0368	25
9000	29
99001	32
99026	35
99023	38
0169	40
98002	43
970172	45
97017	47
98068	50
0375	52
990401	54
99025	58
98023	61

Plan	Page
98075	63
0444	66
0552	69
0275	73
0256	77
0719	80
97023	84
98010	86
98003	88
98042	90
99031	93
99050	95
99040	97
98070	99
97038	103
0049	106
99057	111
0440	114
0033	116
0432	118
99042	121
98050	123
98013	129
97021	131

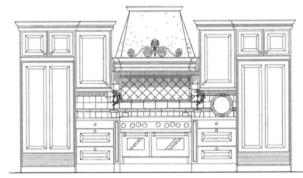

Copyright © 1997-2015 The Kitchen Design Company - All rights reserved

Acknowledgments

To all the Clients I have been fortunate enough to work for.

Because they were willing to make the decision to take a chance on me, that gave me the opportunity to practice my craft, and the confidence to be successful.

The Kitchen Design Company's

Kitchen Idea Book

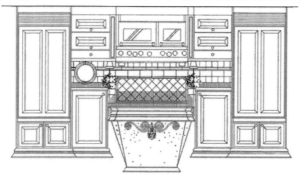

Copyright © 1997-2015 The Kitchen Design Company - All rights reserved

Introduction

This book contains fifty plans and 3D perspective drawings. **To use this book,** simply thumb through and mark all the plans and perspective elements you like and want in your kitchen. Take these drawings to your kitchen designer, architect, or interior designer and have them modified to fit your specific space and needs. Or we can do it for you. It's that simple.

If you find kitchen plans or perspectives you would like larger scale (1/2" = 1'-0") 22"x 17" size copies are available. You can purchase them for any of the kitchens shown by following the instructions at the back of this book.

You can also purchase Kitchen Interior Design Drawings (KIDD) consisting of dimensioned Floor Plan, dimensioned Interior Elevations, and 3D Perspective Drawings for any of the 50 kitchens shown. All KIDD sets are drawn at 1/2" = 1'-0" scale, and the drawing sheet size is 22" x 17".

To see an example of a Kitchen Interior Design Drawings set, go to www.KitchenDesignCo.com/ then go to the bottom of the page. Under Kitchen Design Drawings click on Kitchen Interior Design Drawings to see a complete KIDD set.

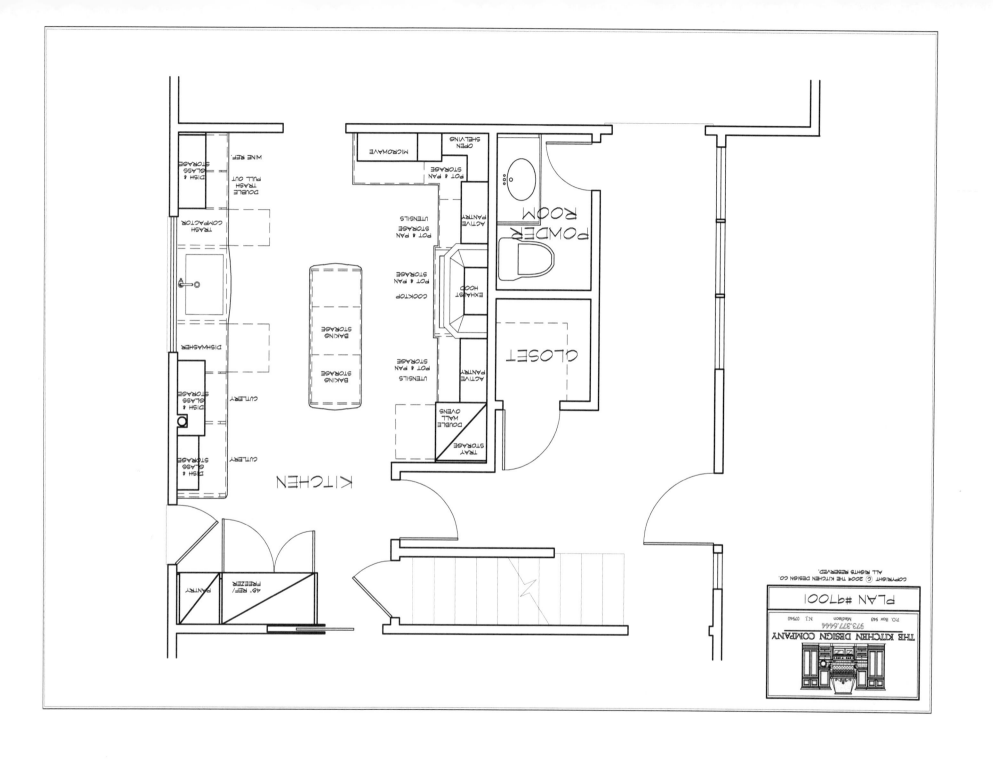

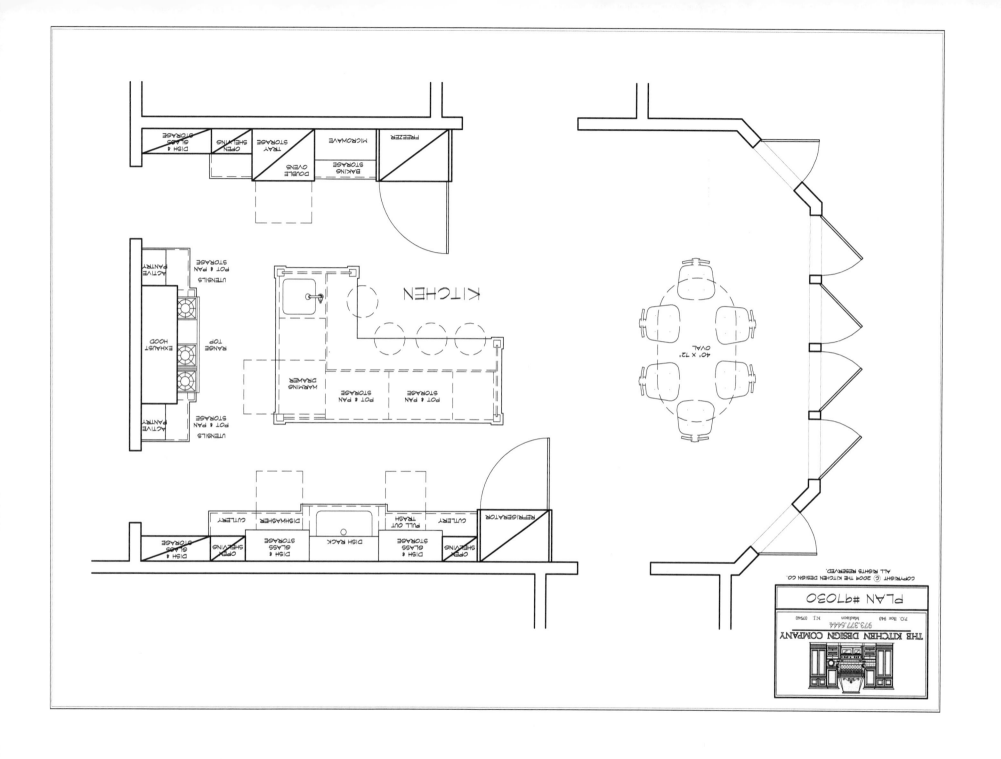

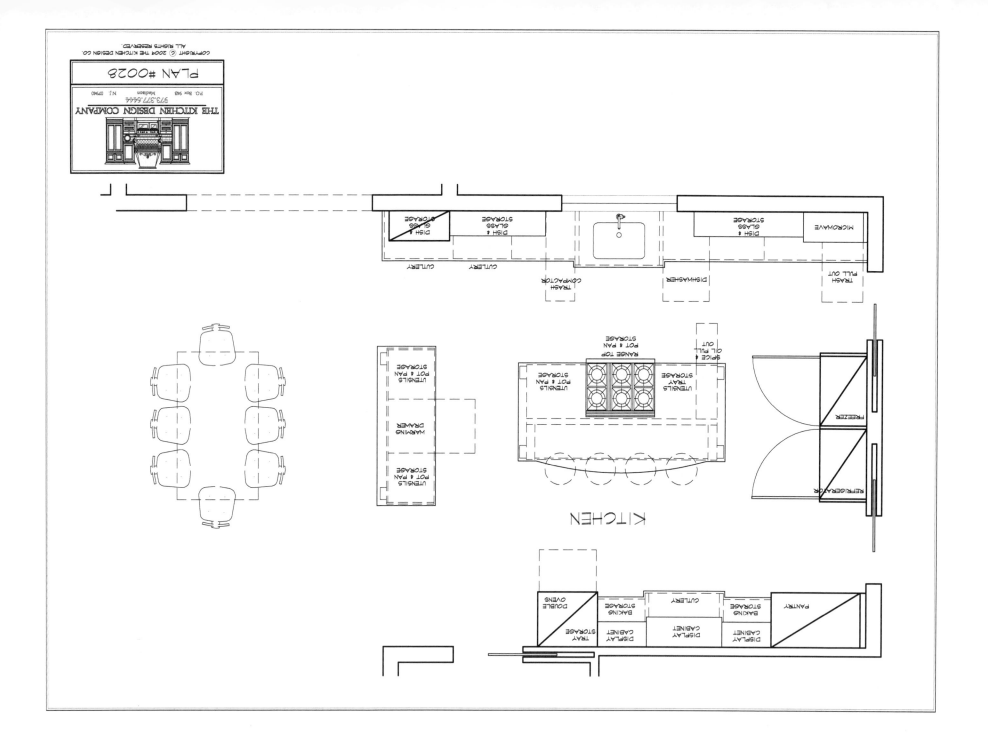

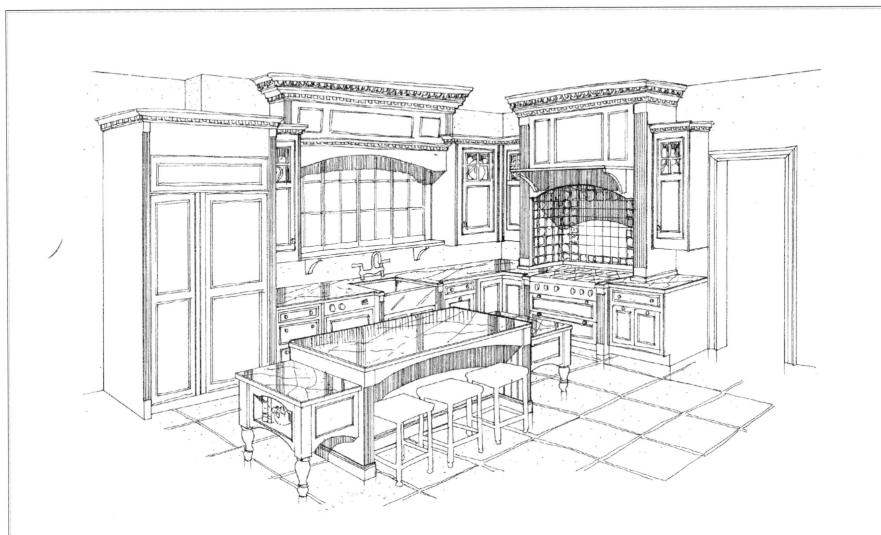

PLAN #97020

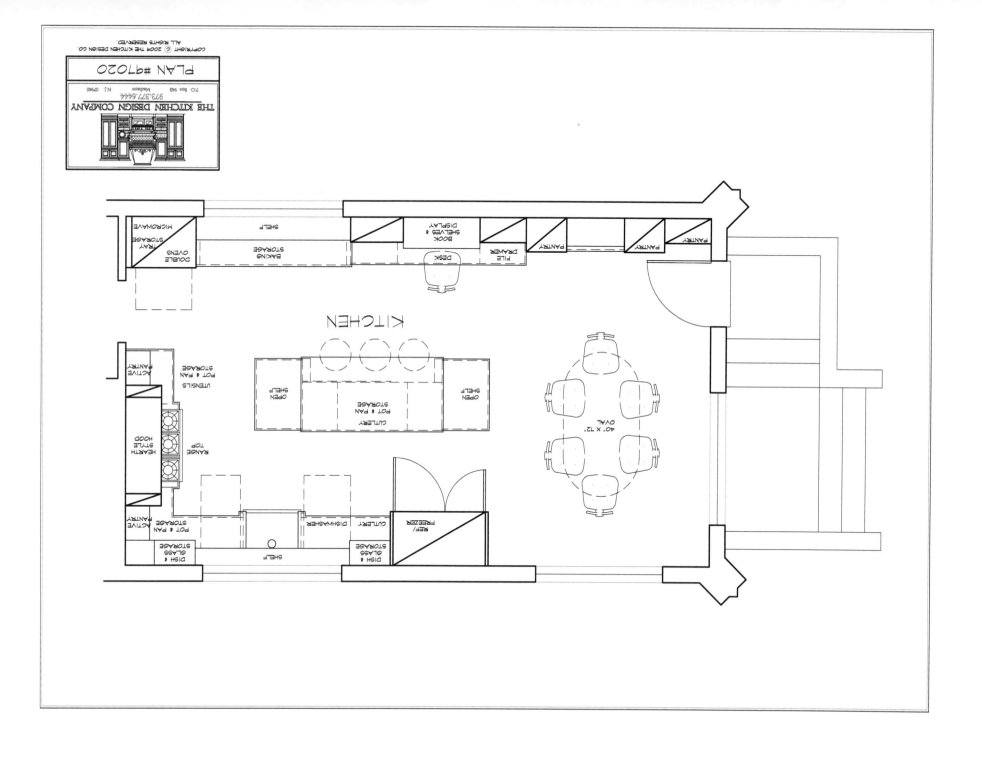

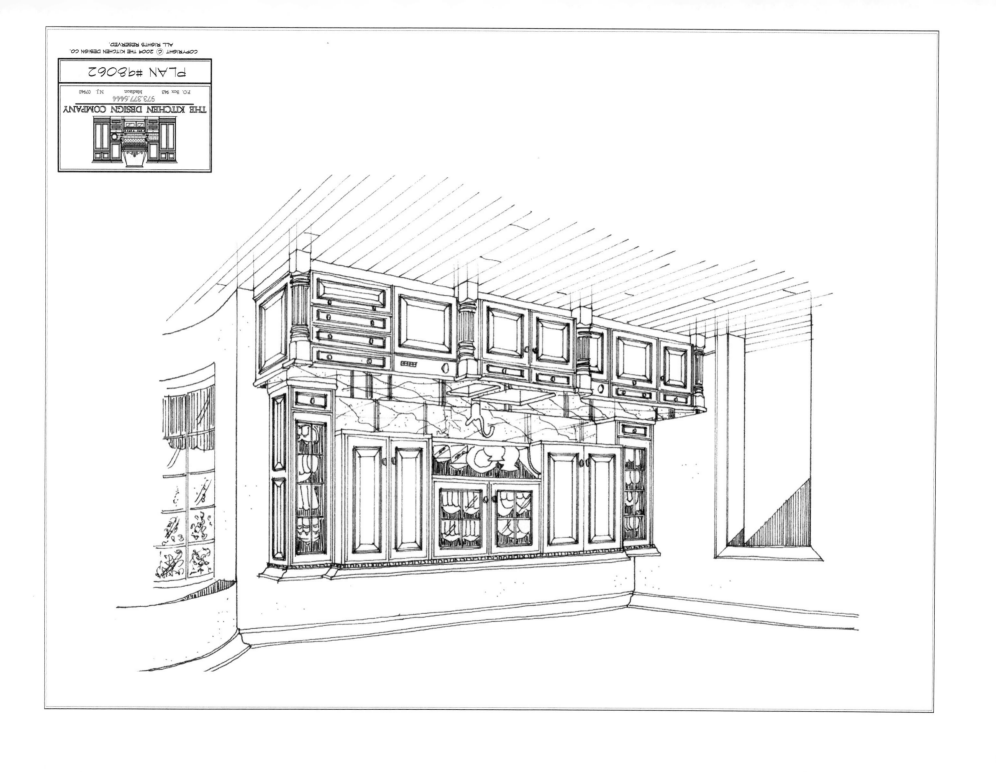

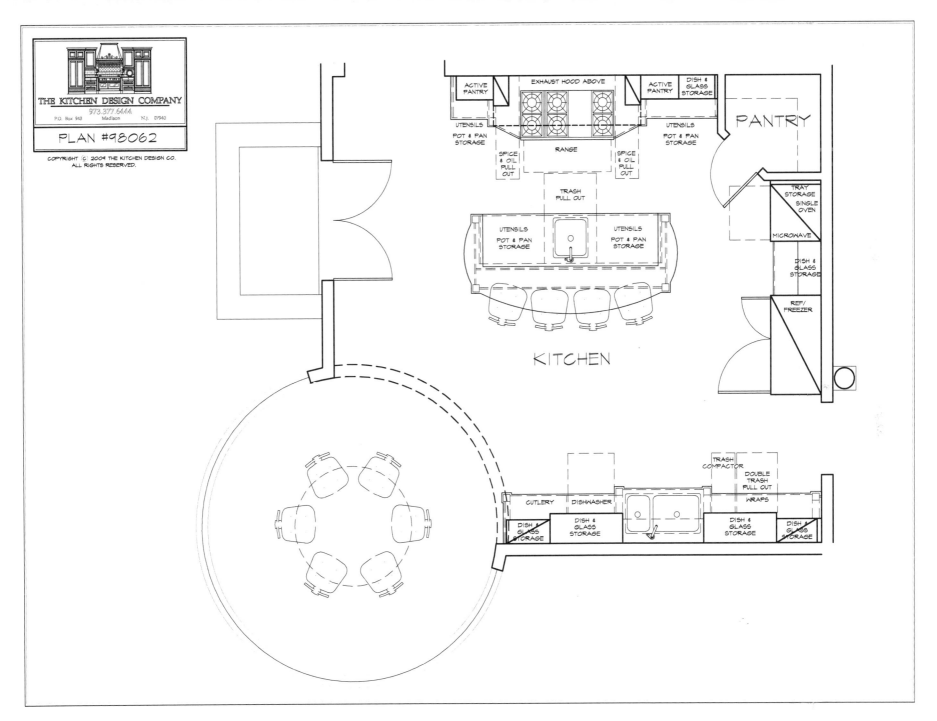

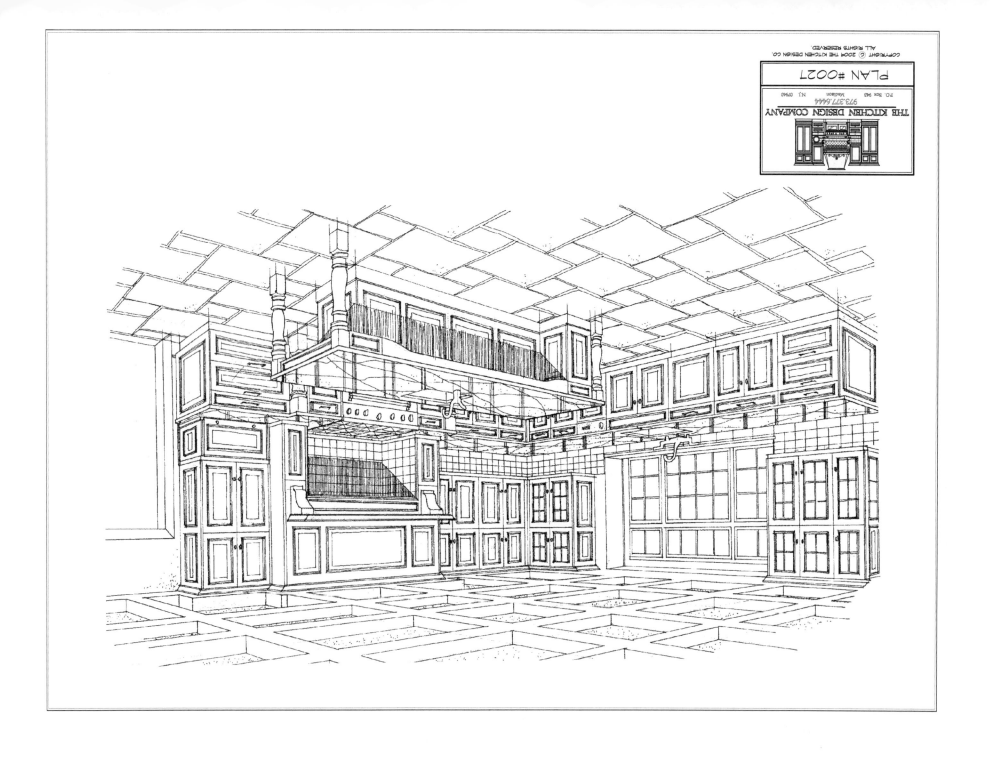

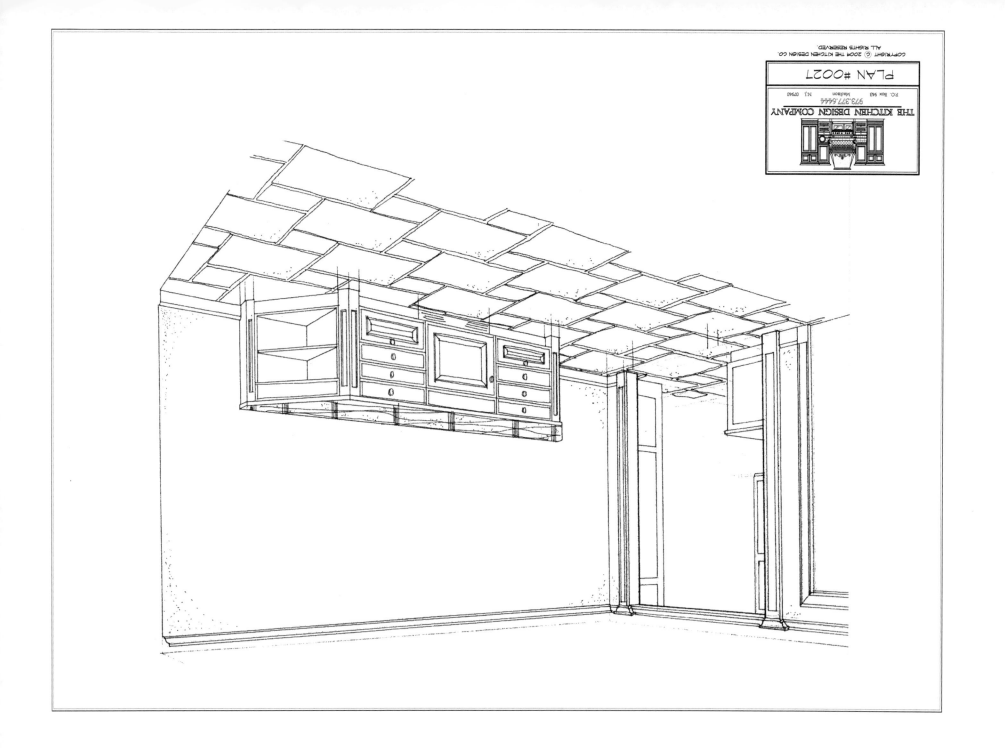

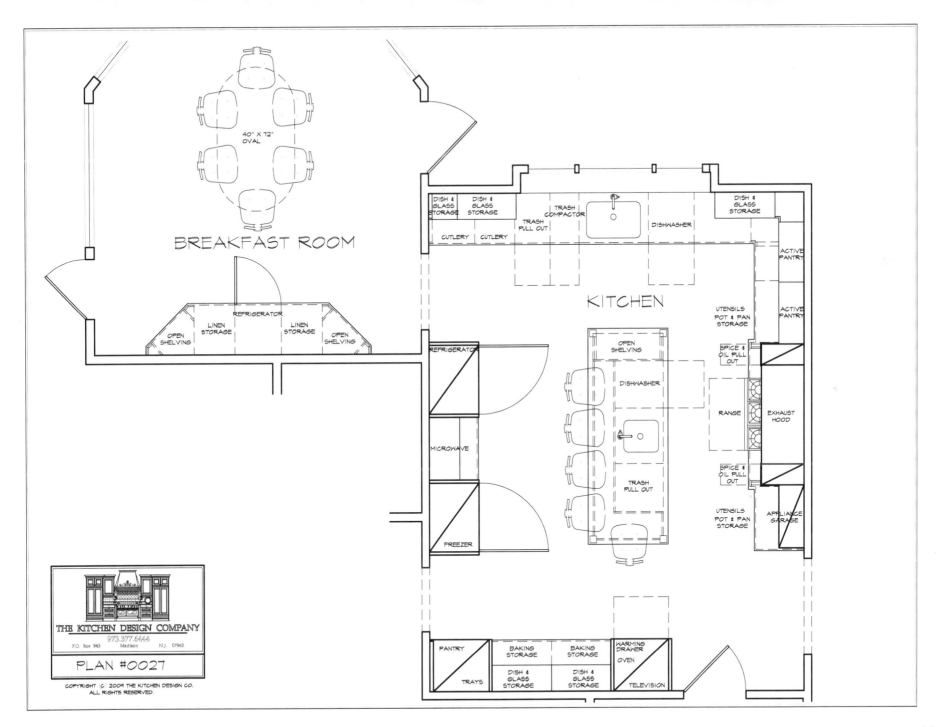

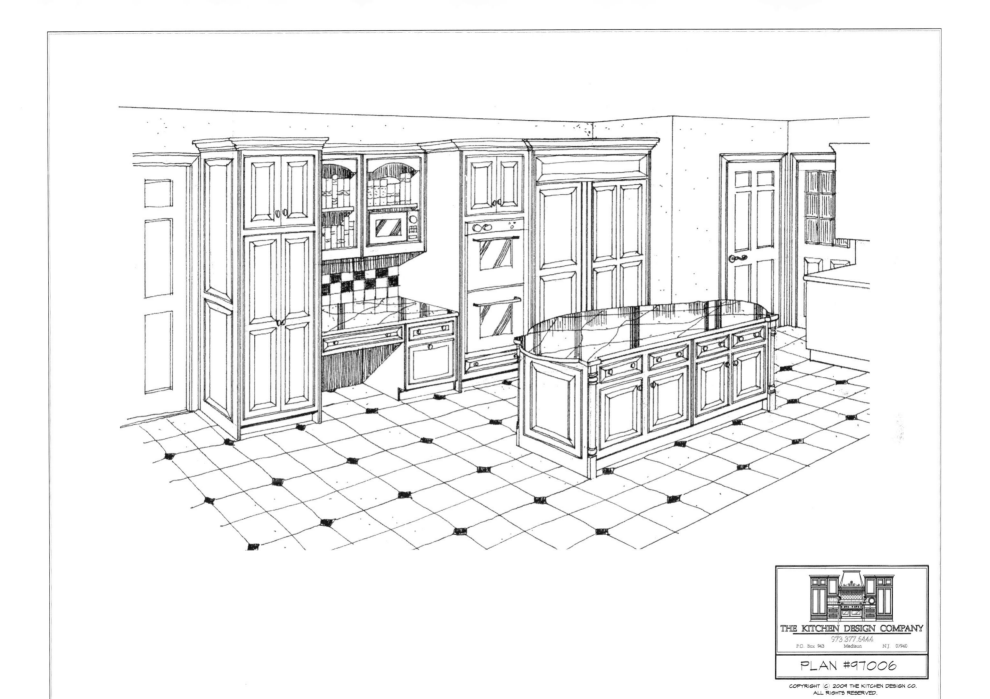

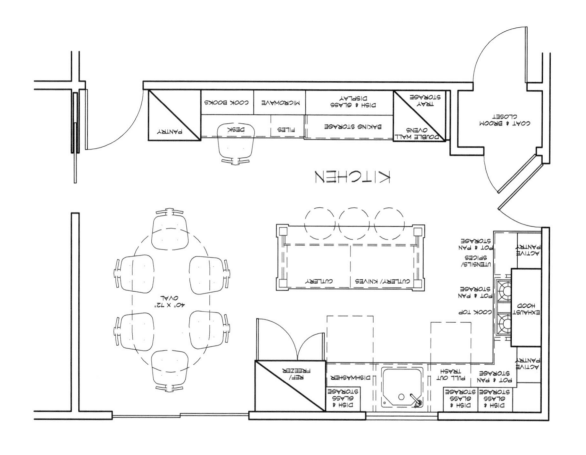

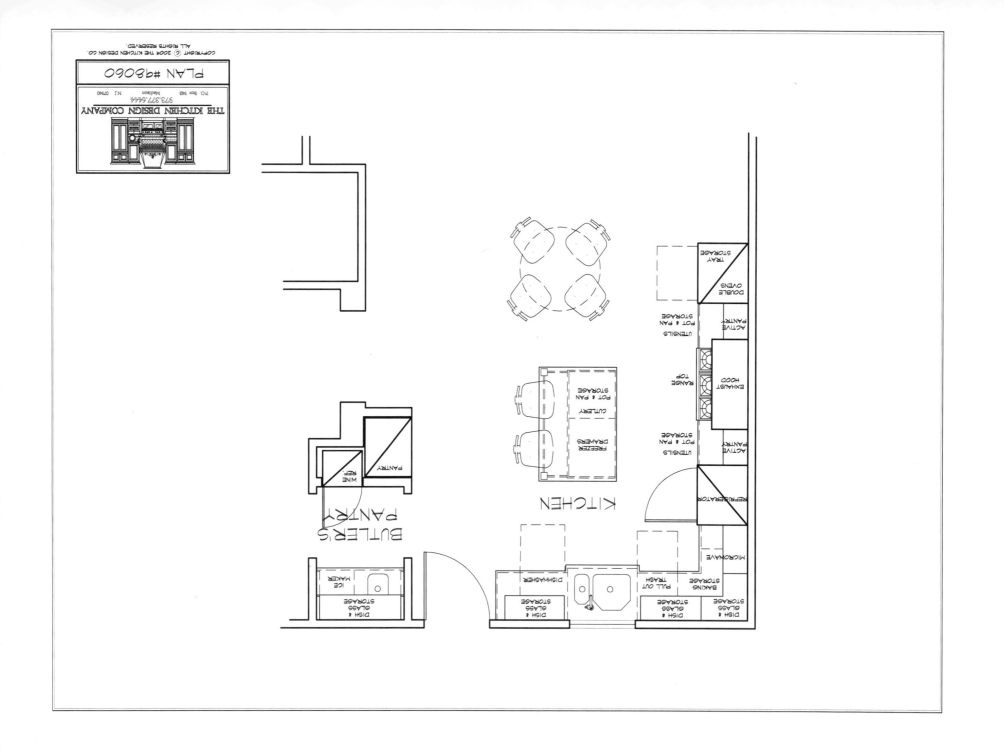

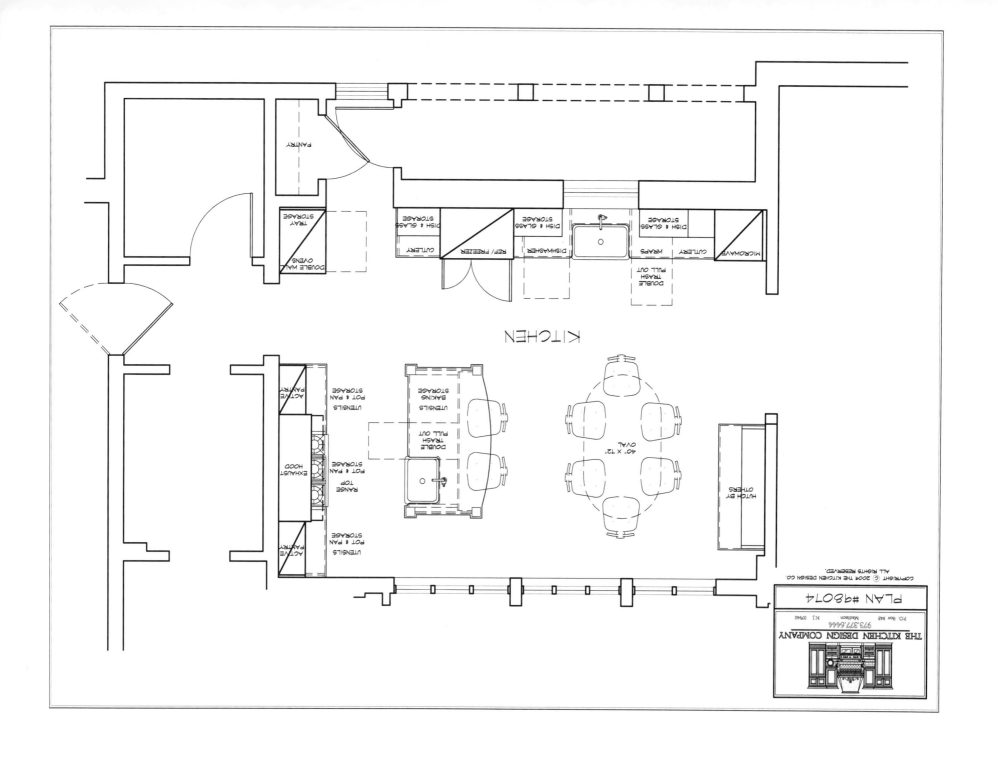

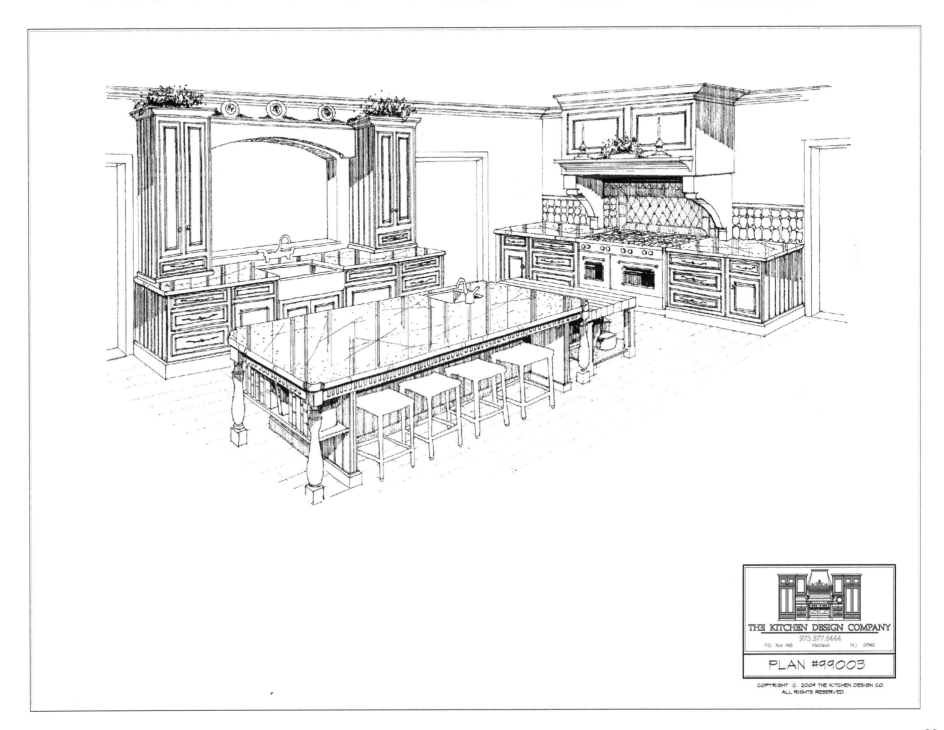

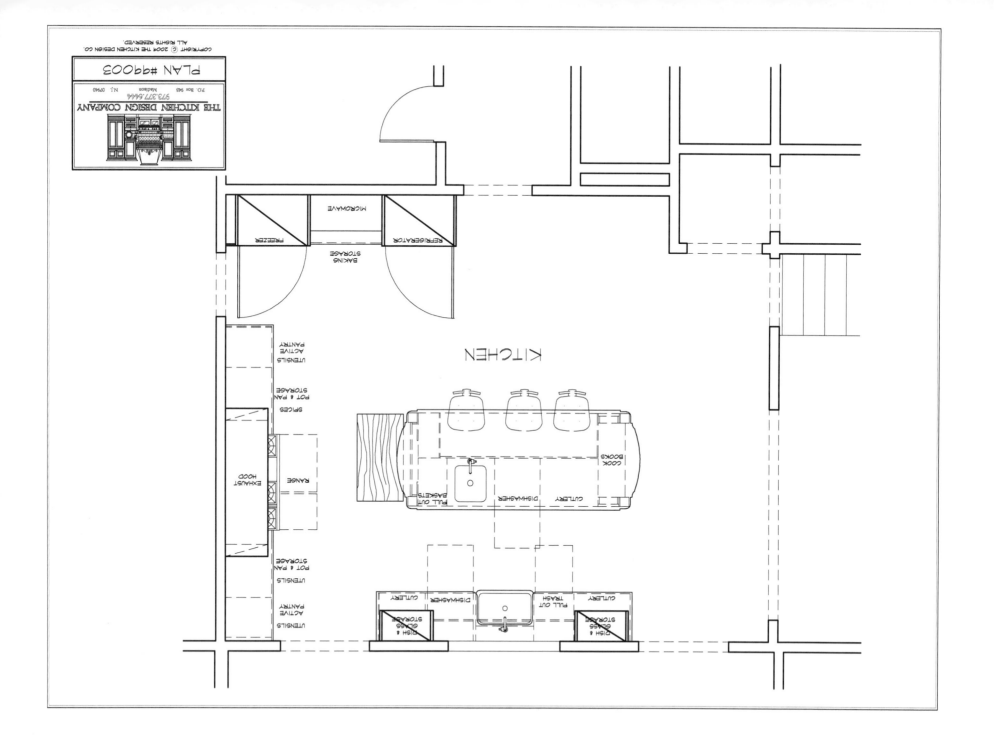

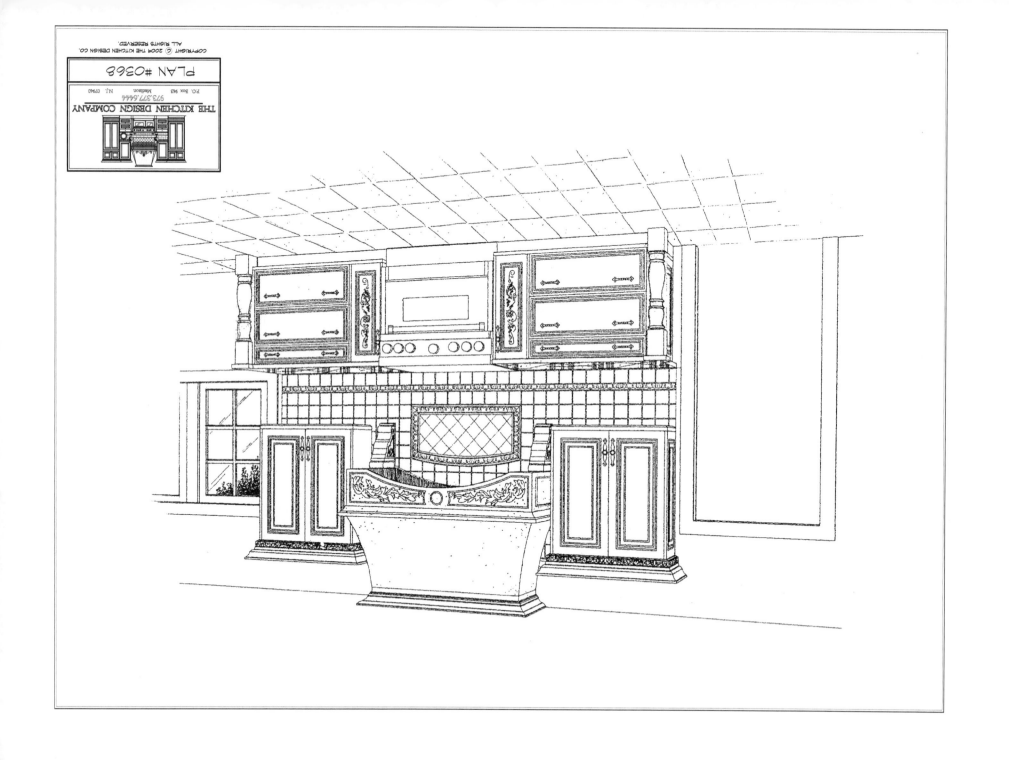

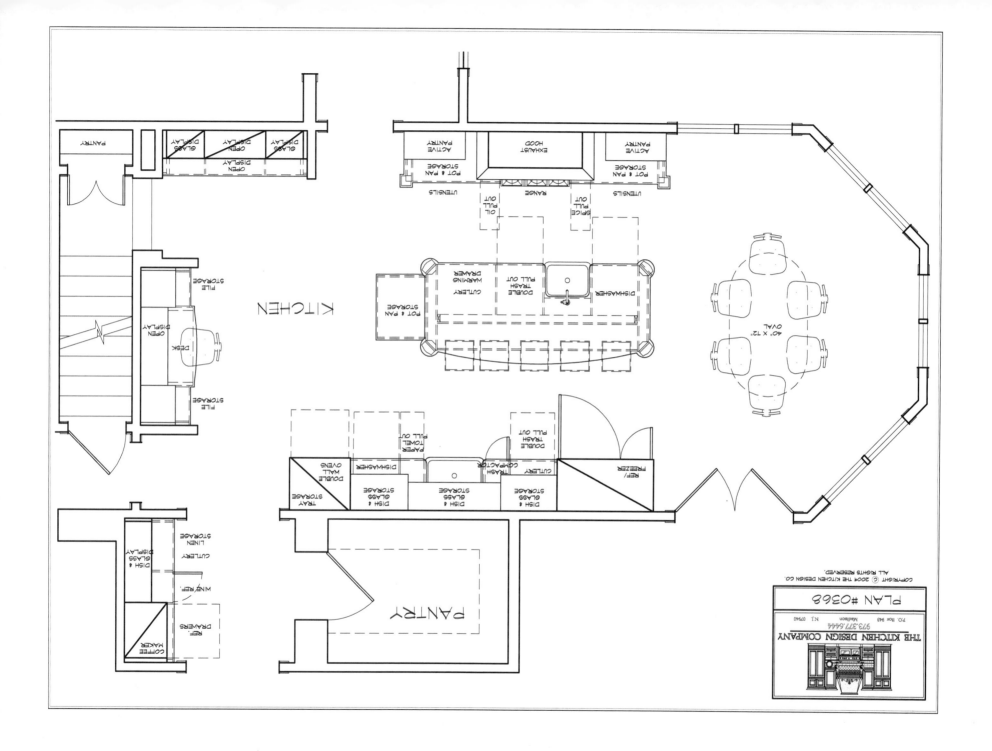

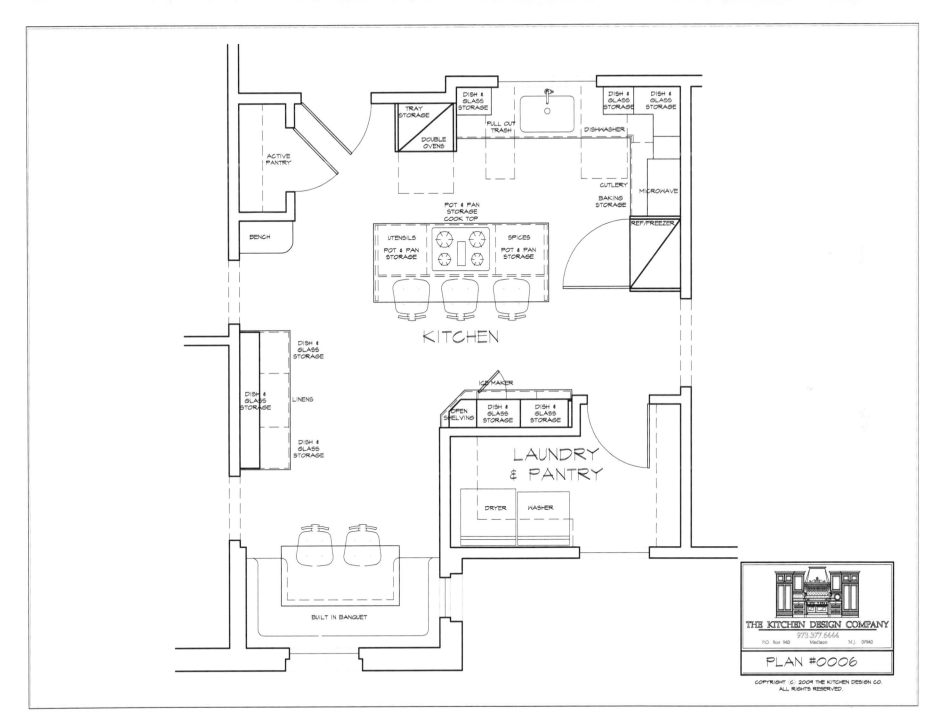

PLAN #0006

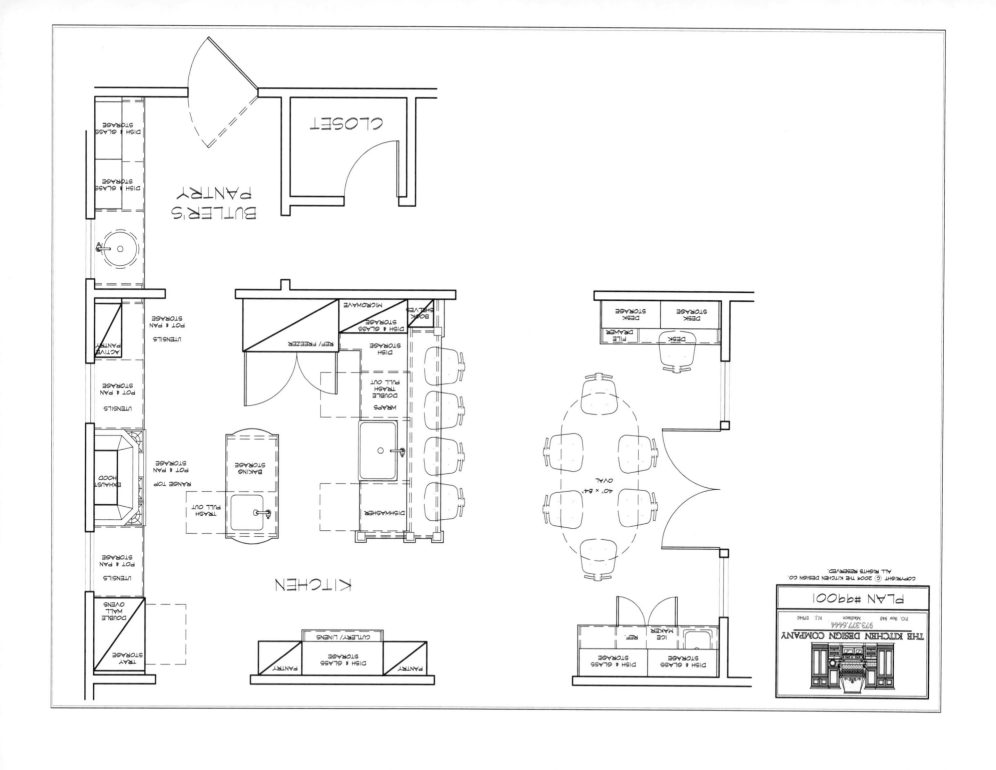

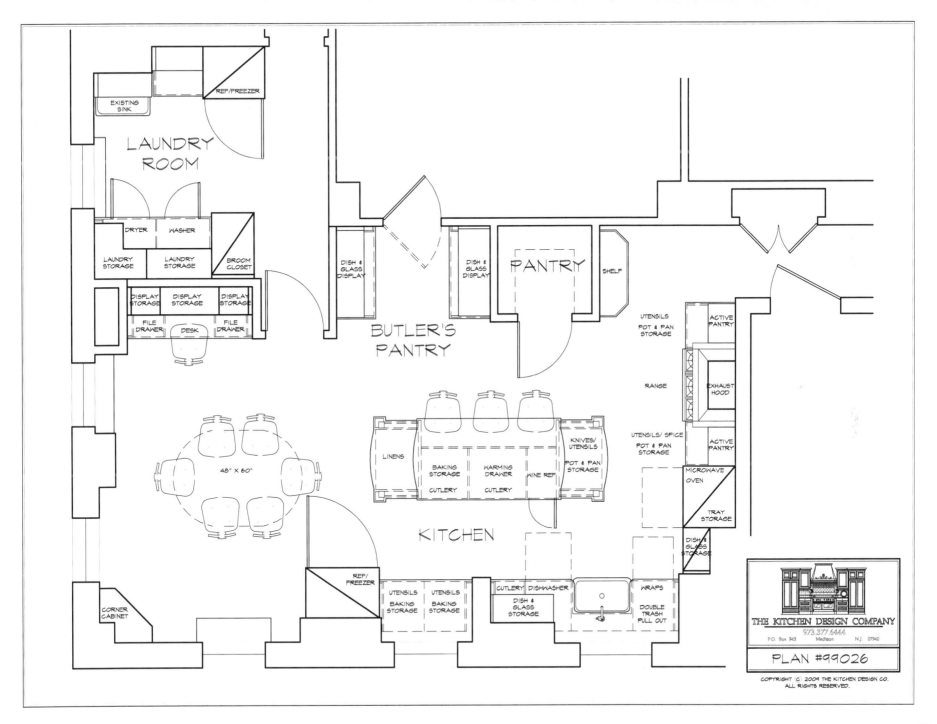

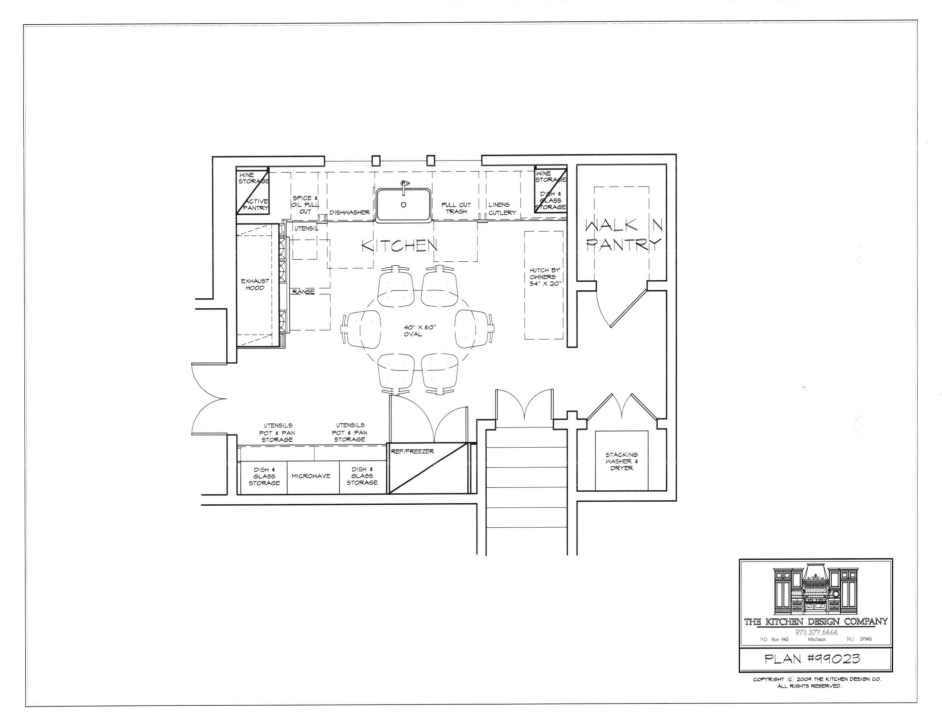

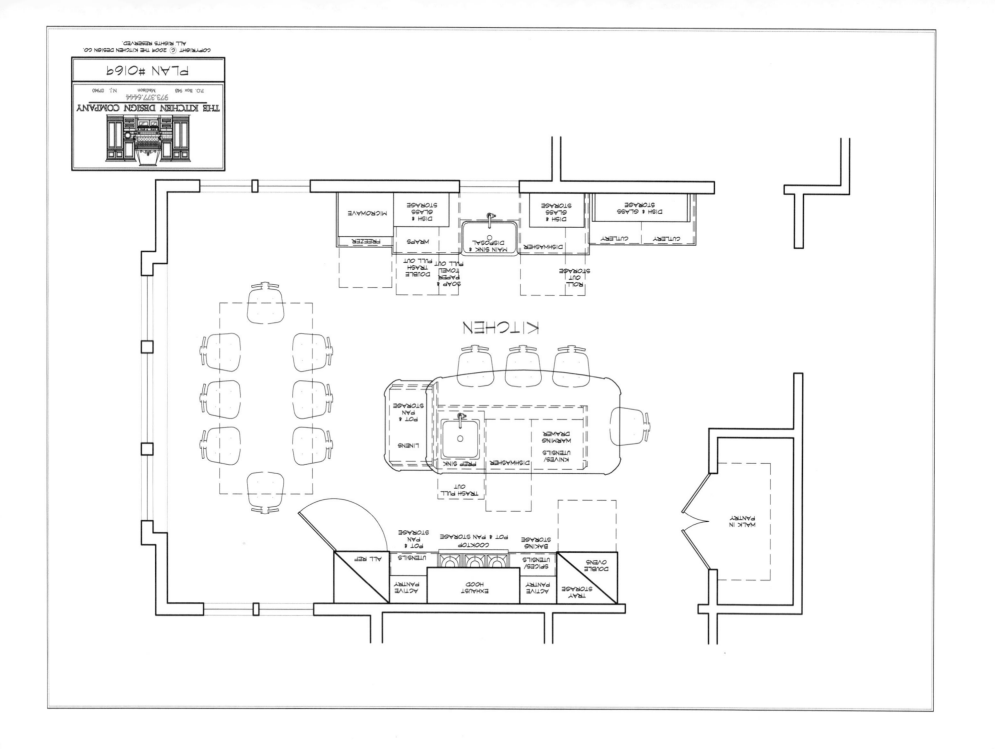

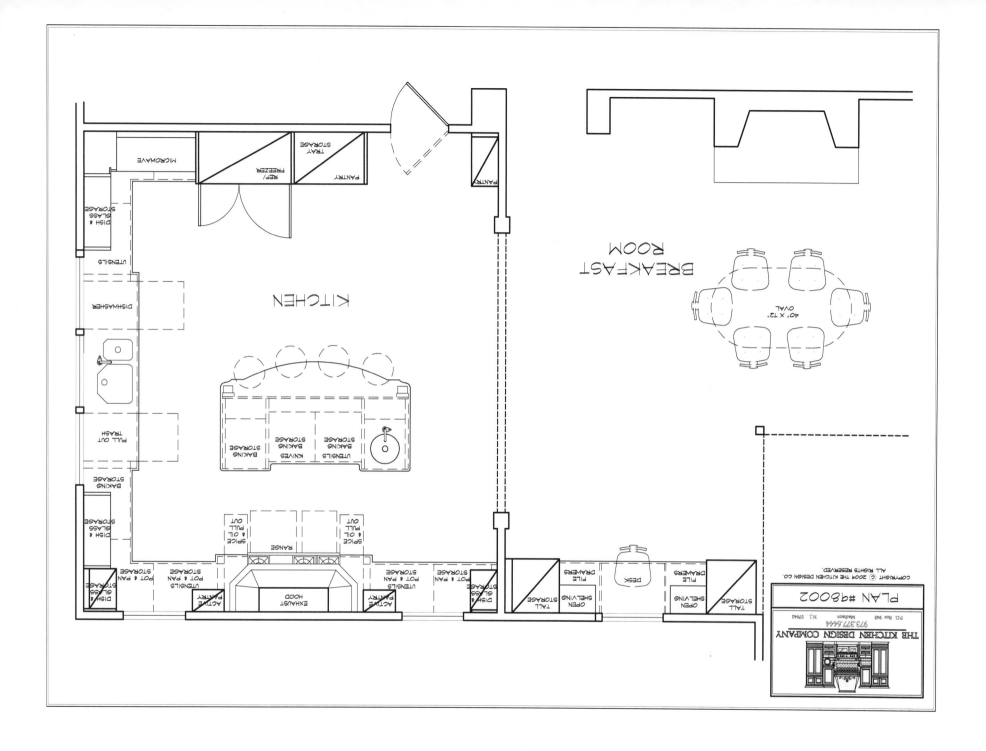

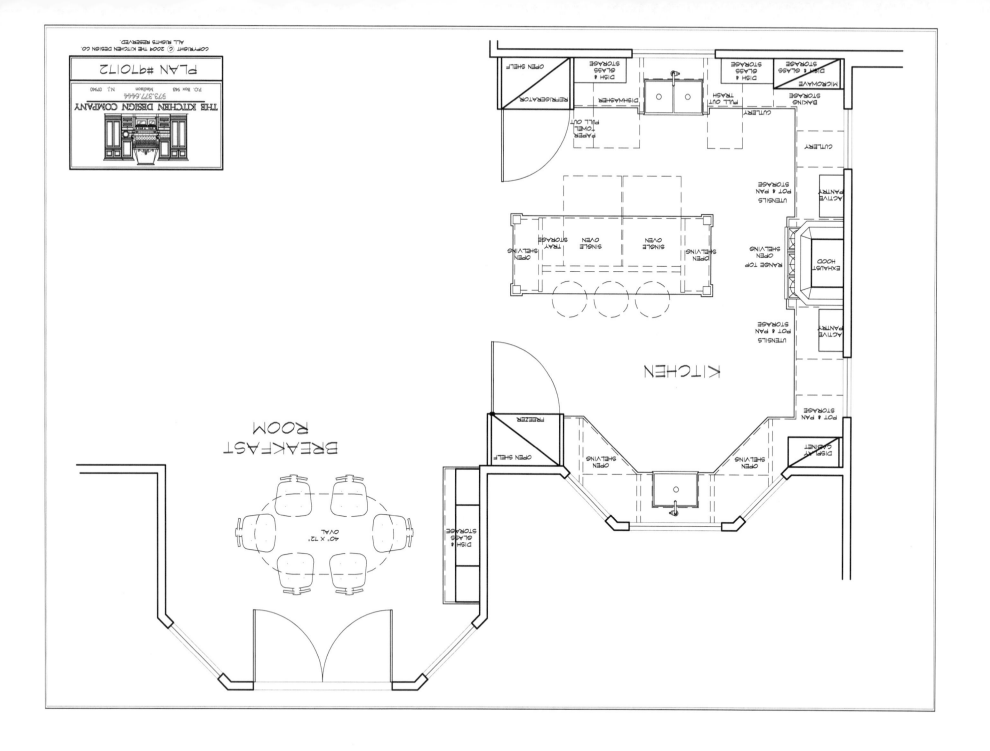

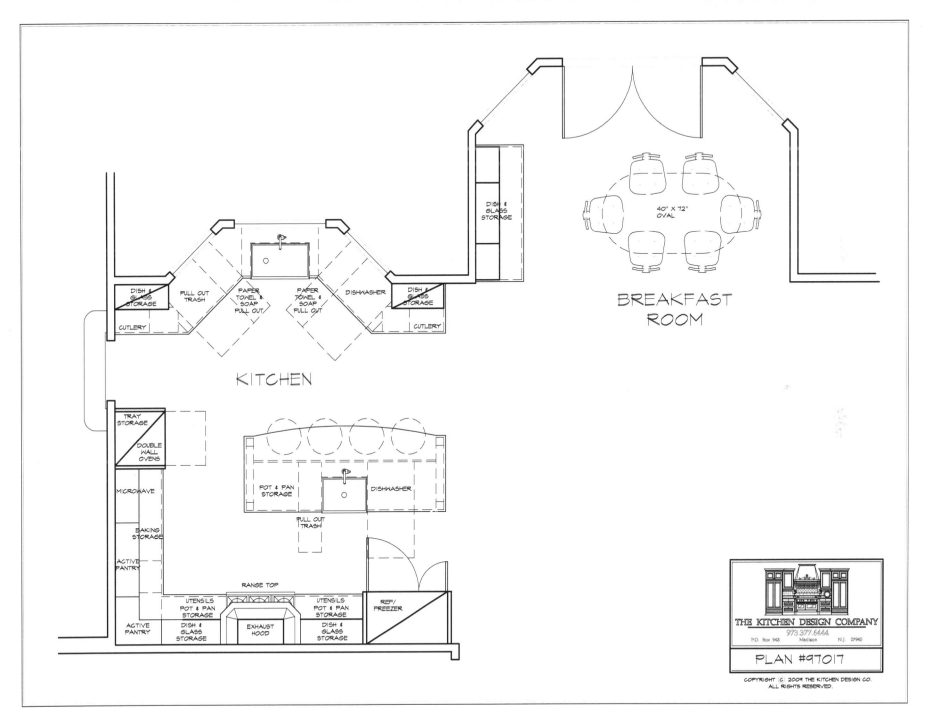

PLAN #98068

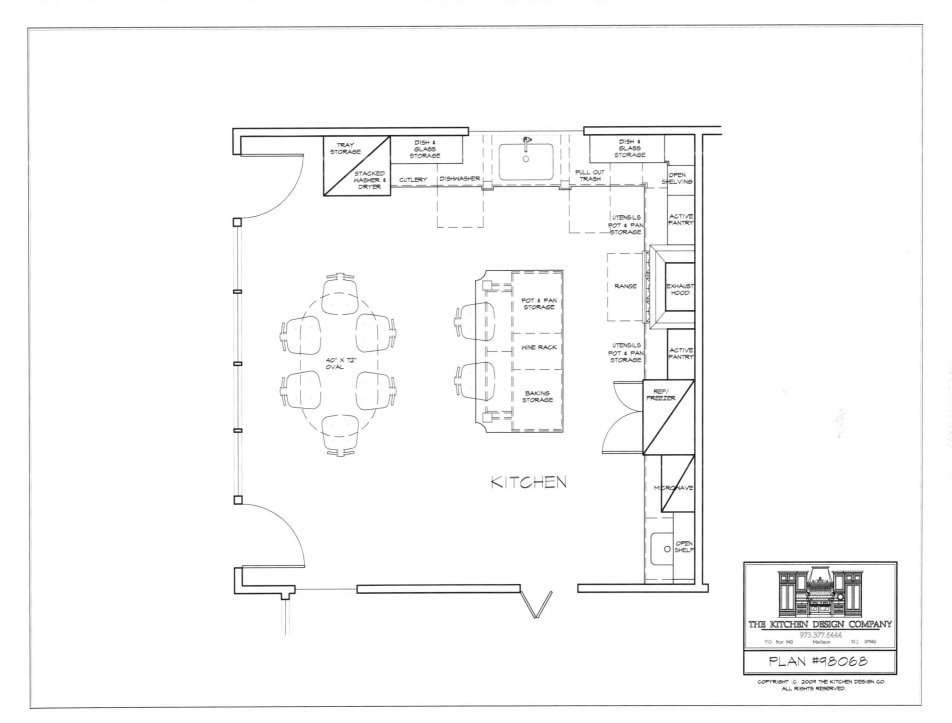

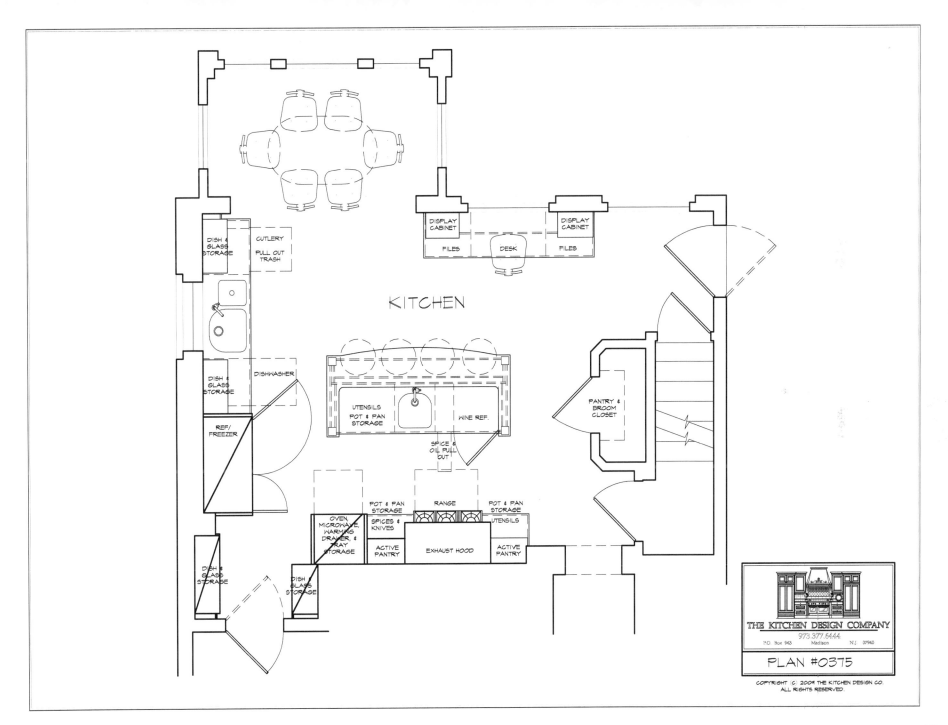

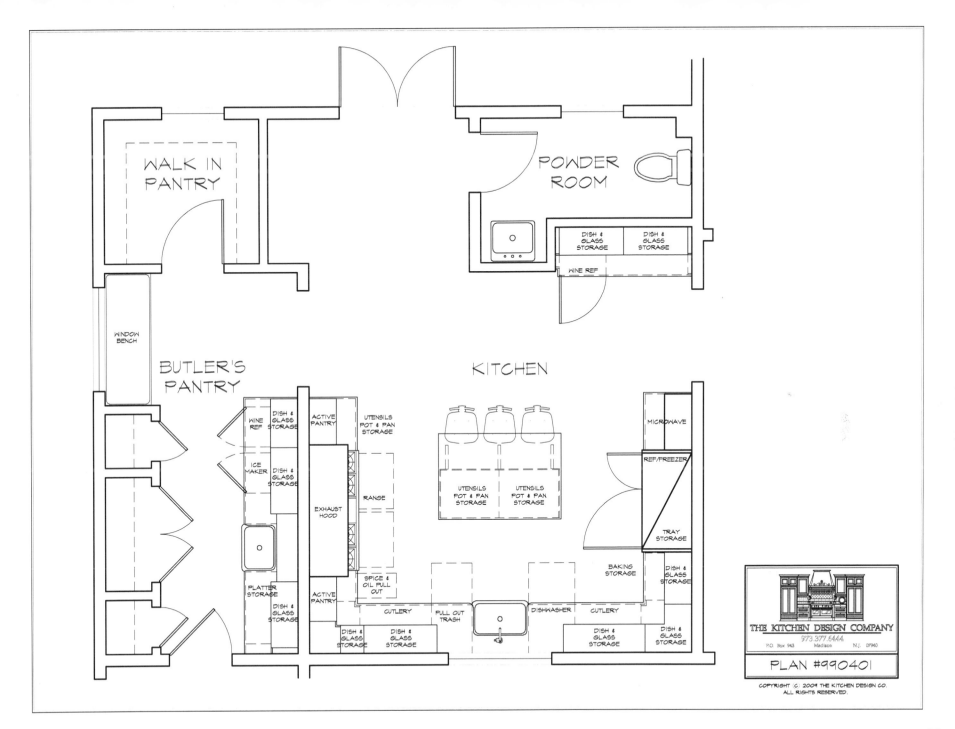

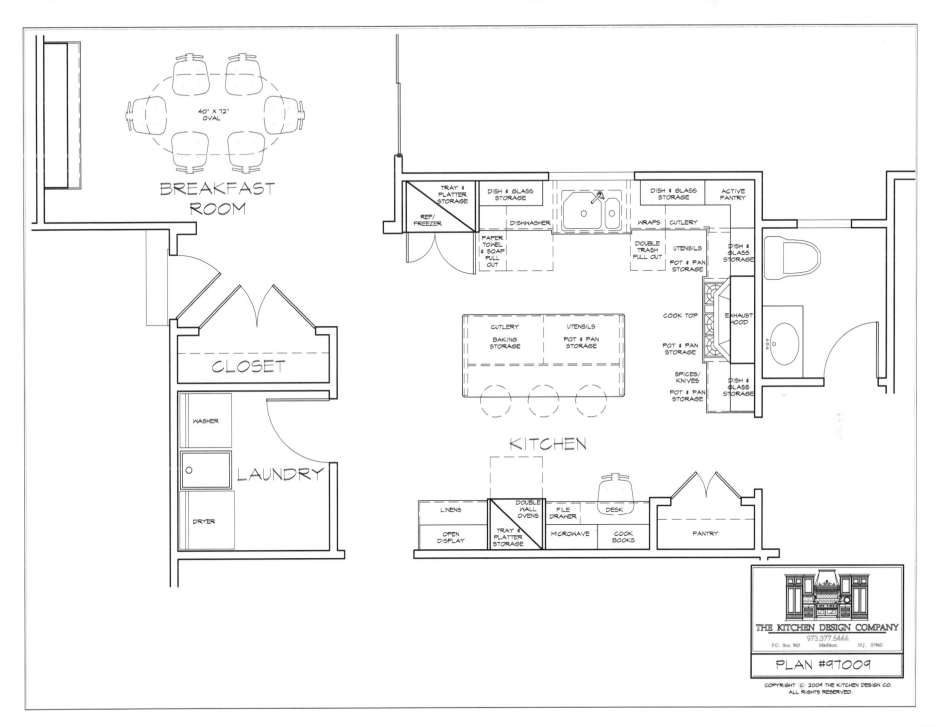

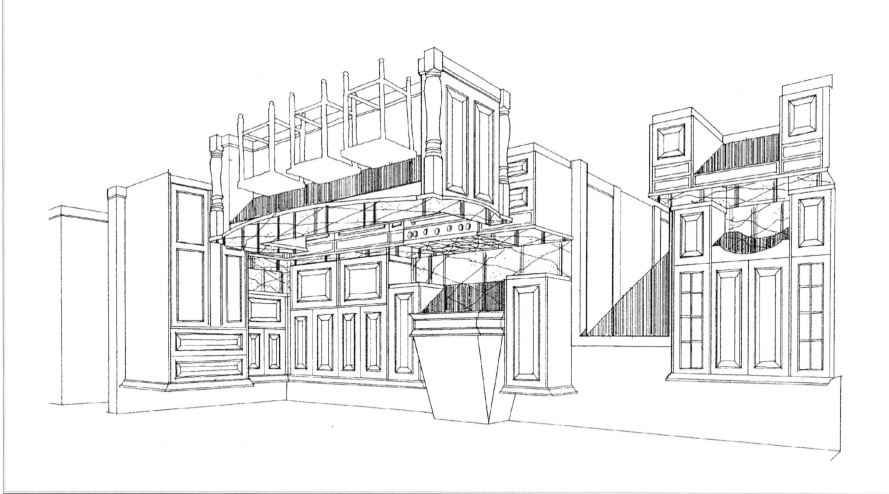

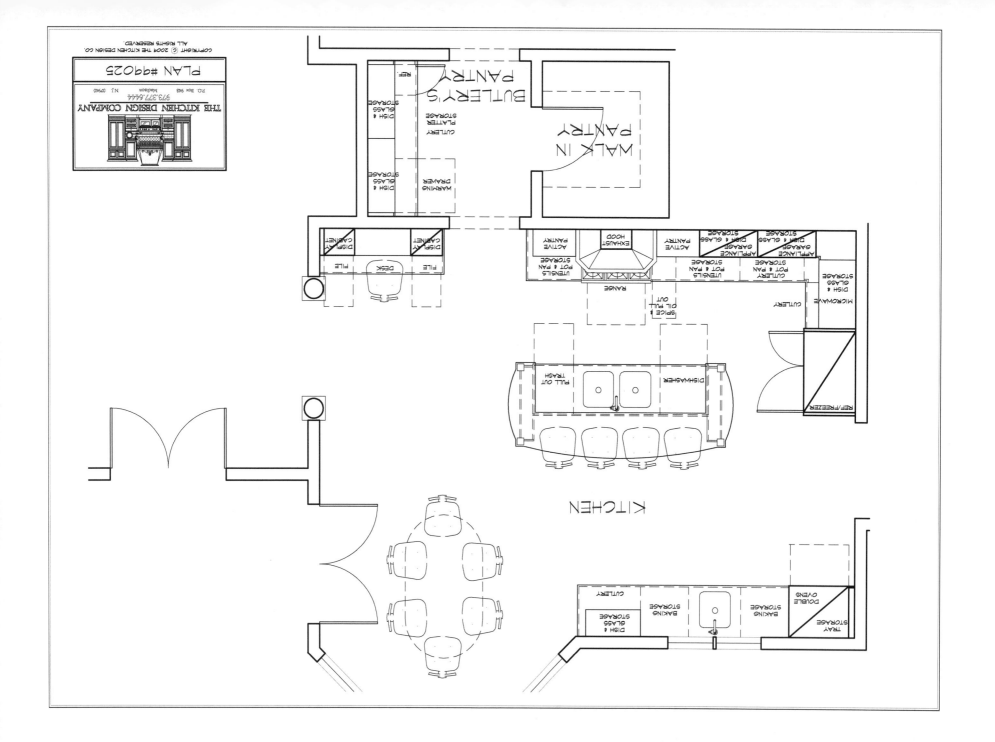

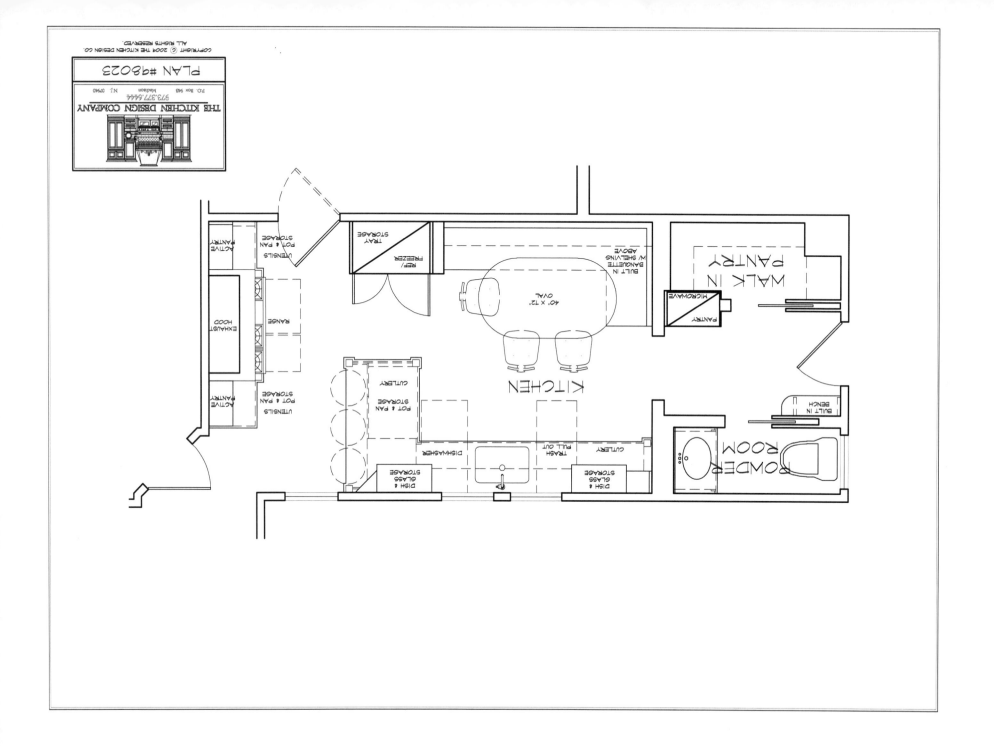

PLAN #98075

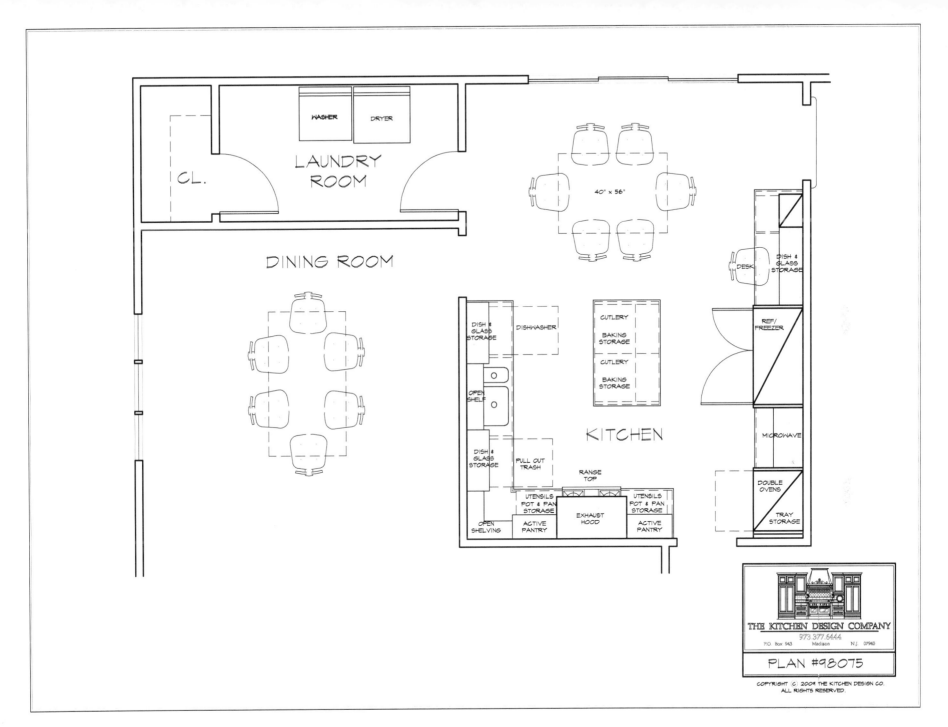

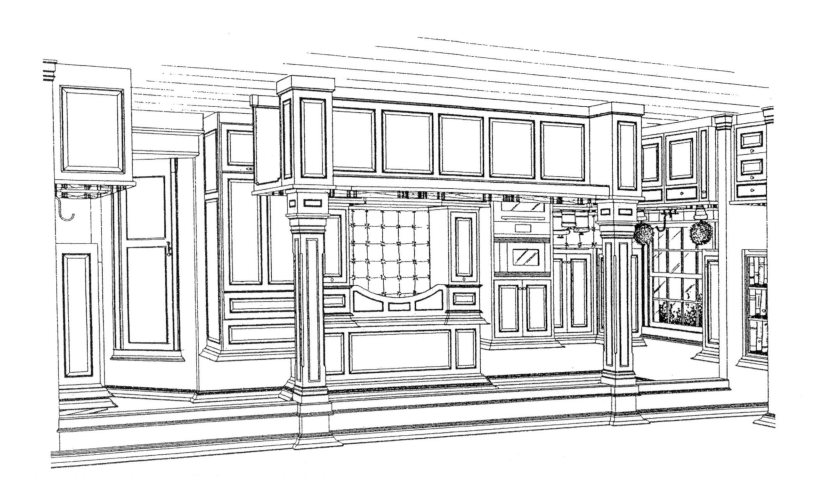

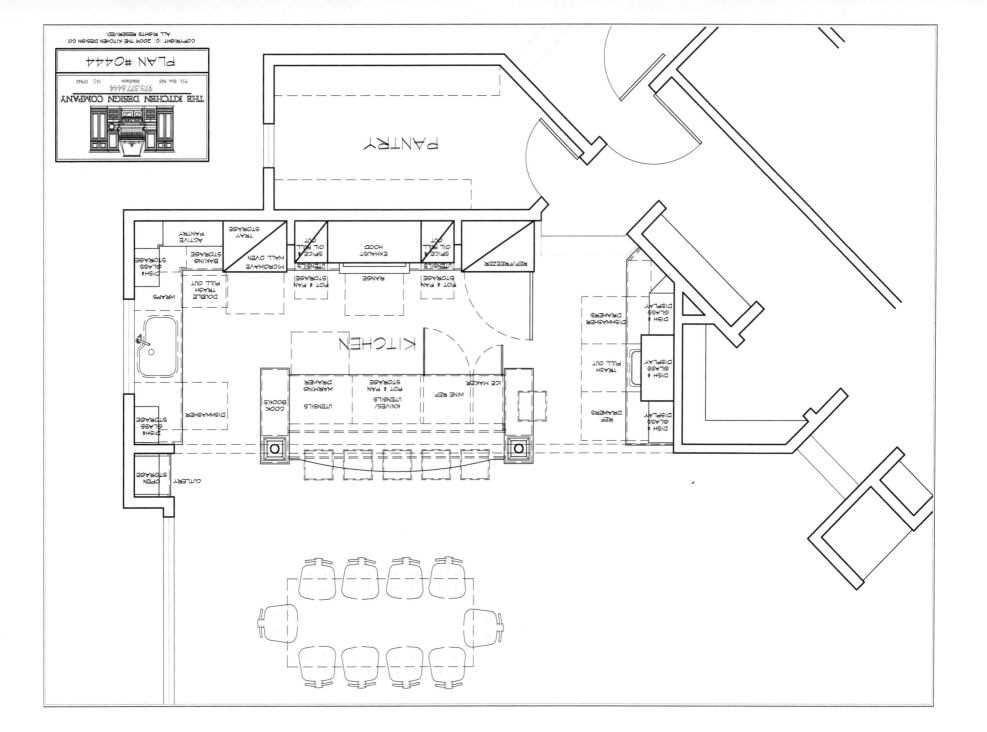

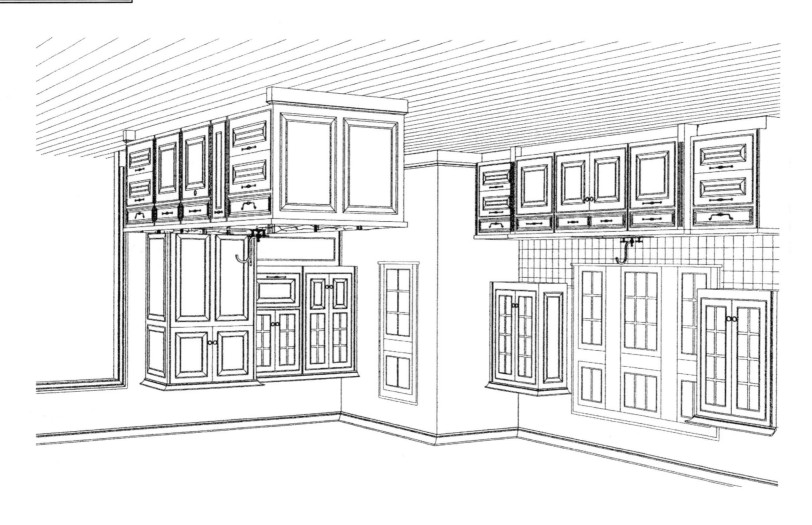

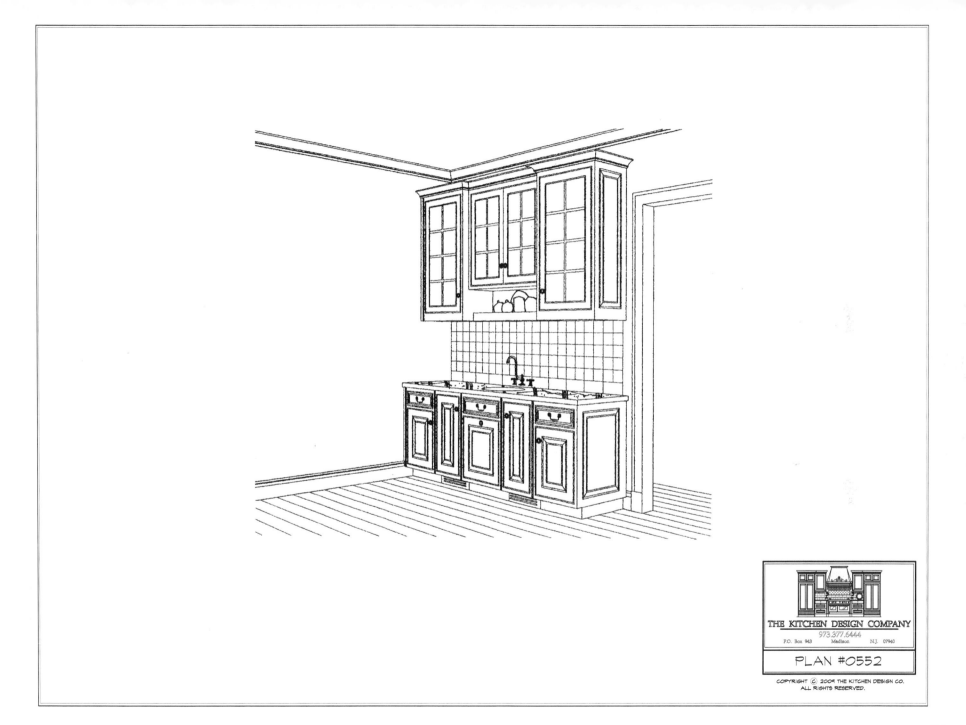

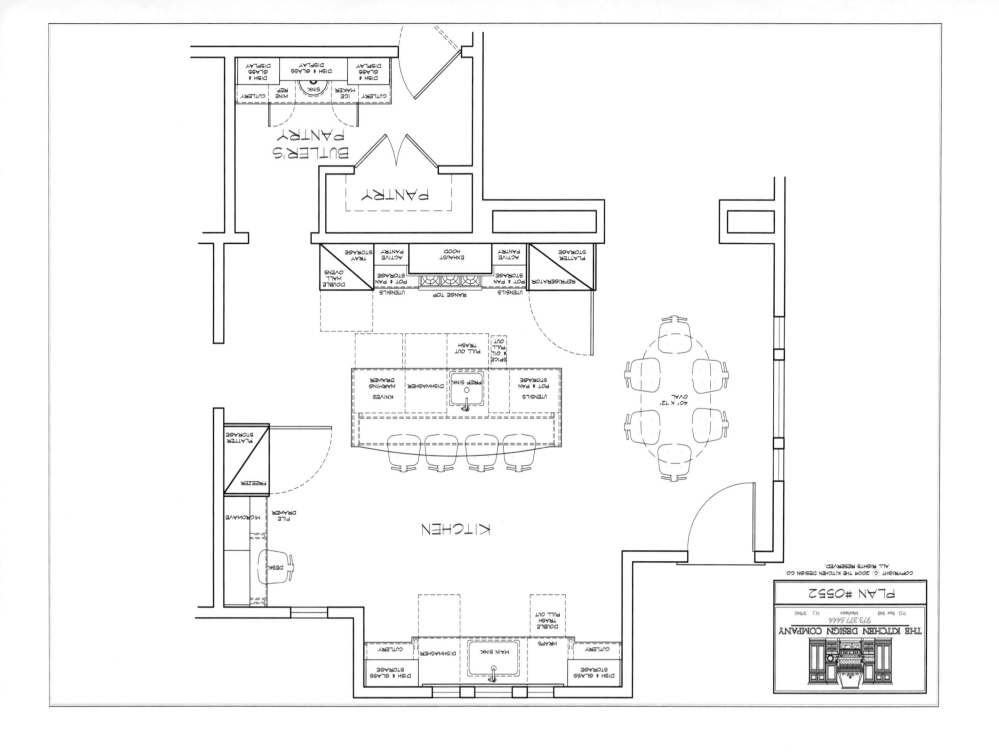

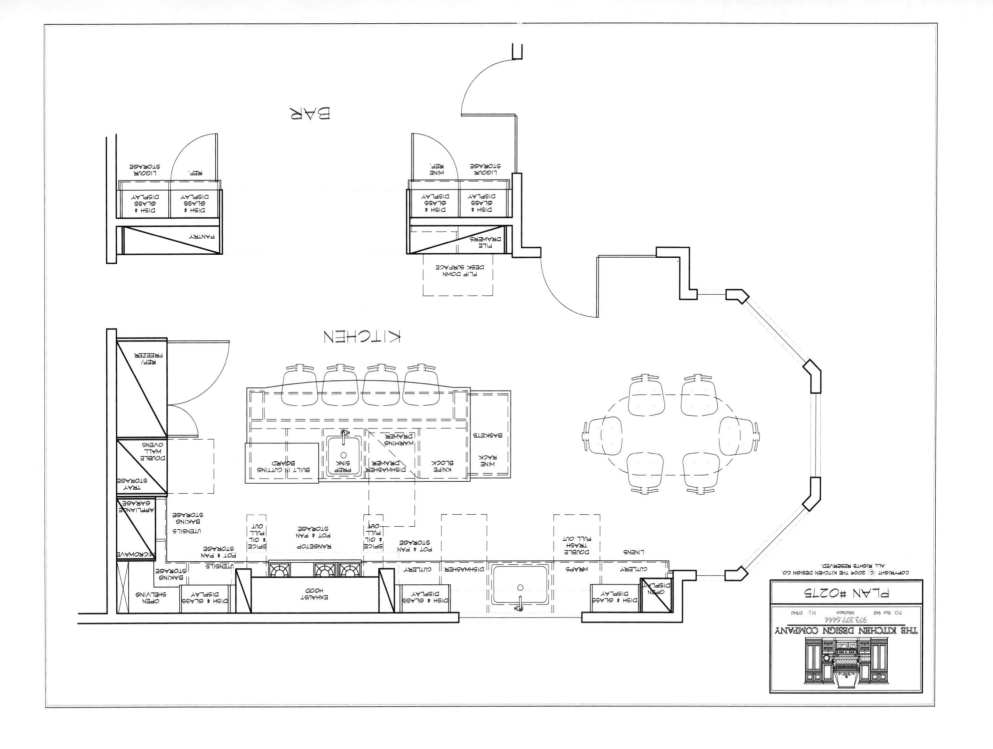

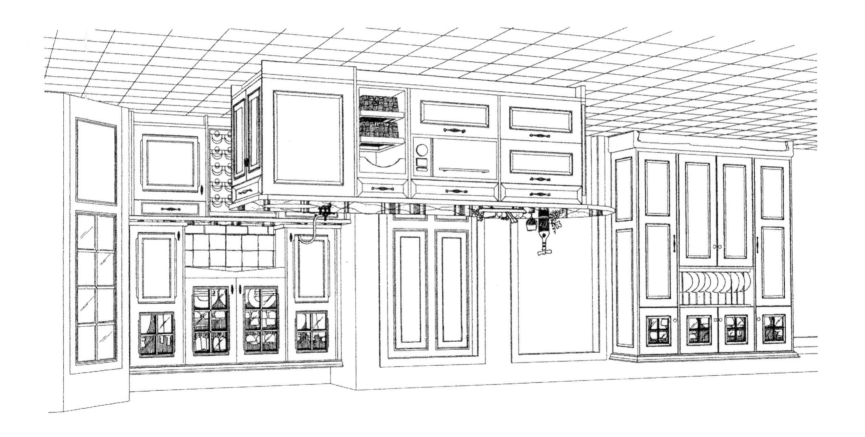

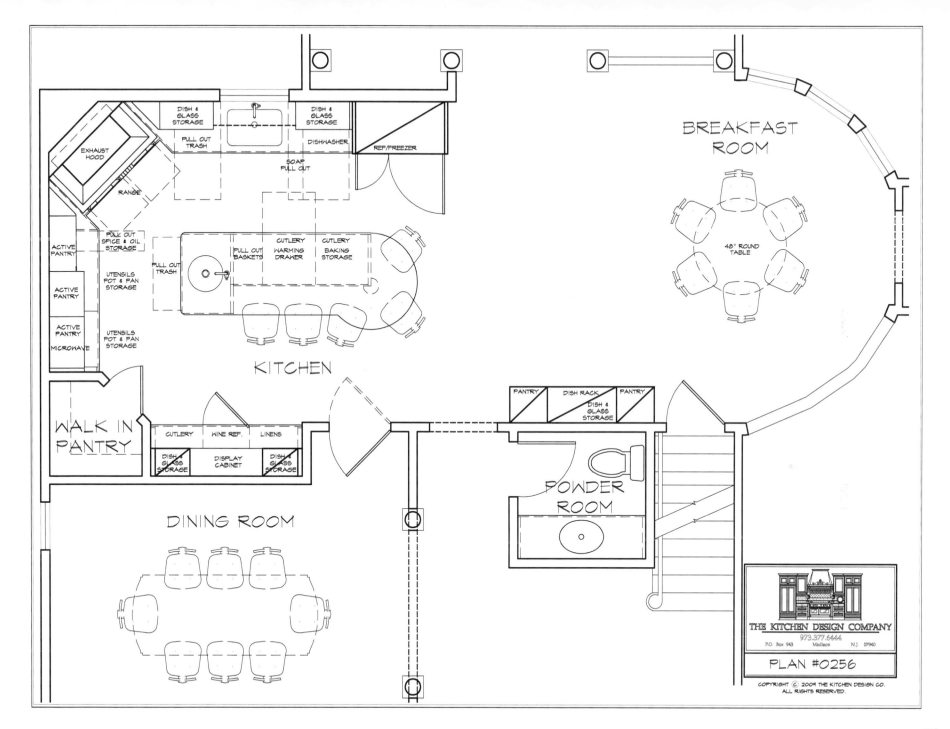

THE KITCHEN DESIGN COMPANY
973.377.6444
P.O. Box 943　Madison, NJ 07940

PLAN #0719

COPYRIGHT (C) 2004 THE KITCHEN DESIGN CO.
ALL RIGHTS RESERVED.

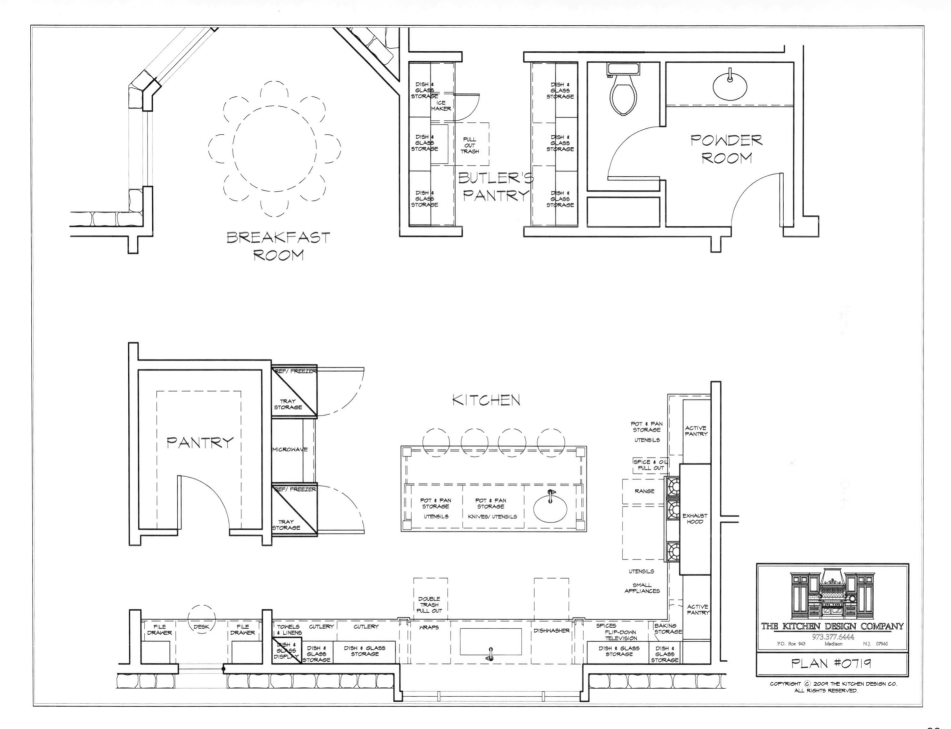

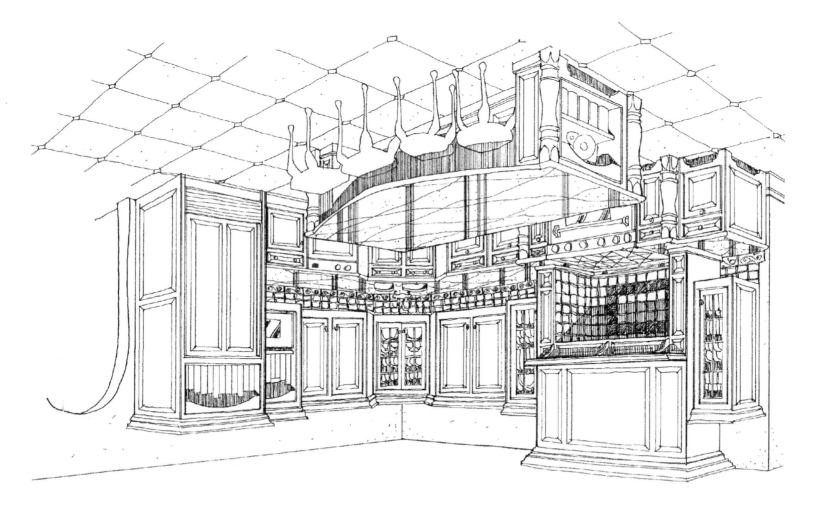

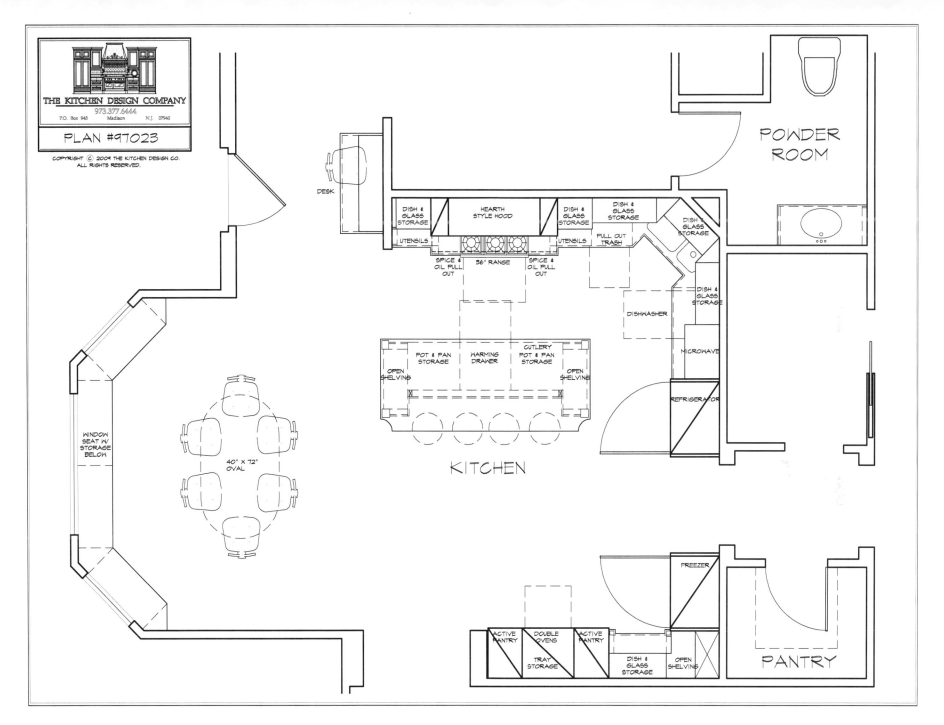

PLAN #98010

THE KITCHEN DESIGN COMPANY

P.O. Box 543   Madison, N.J. 07940
973.377.6444

COPYRIGHT (C) 2004 THE KITCHEN DESIGN CO. ALL RIGHTS RESERVED.

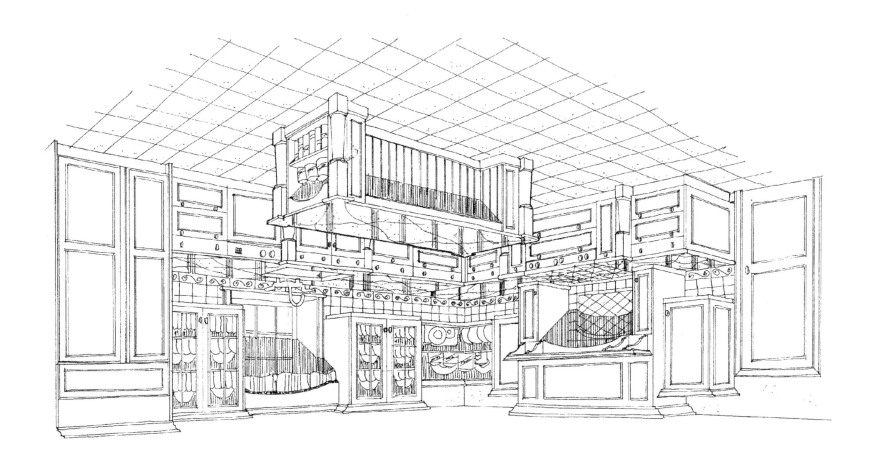

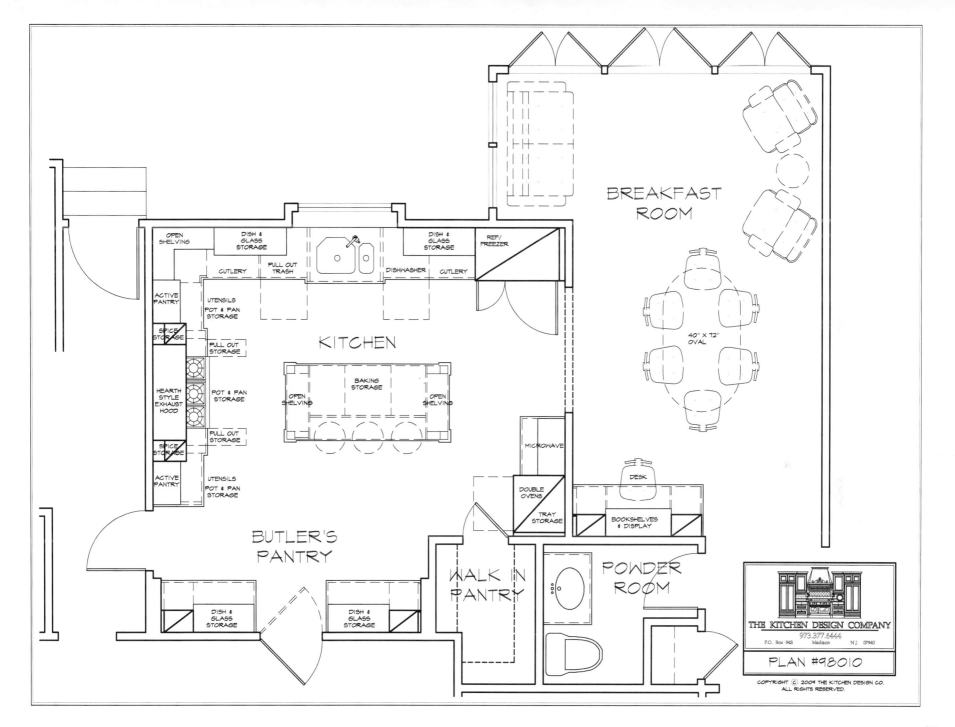

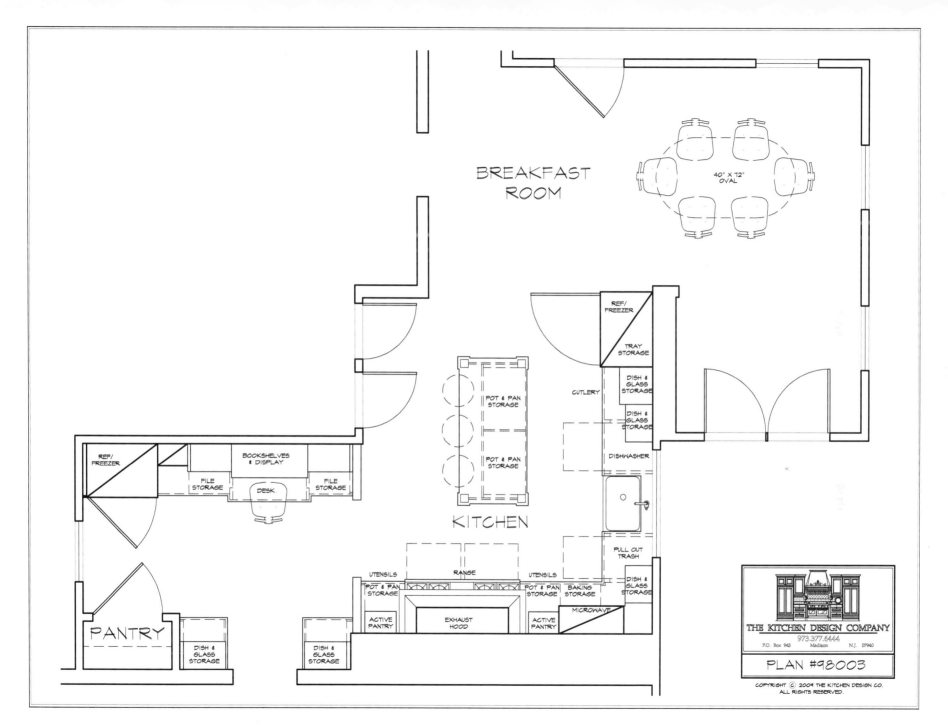

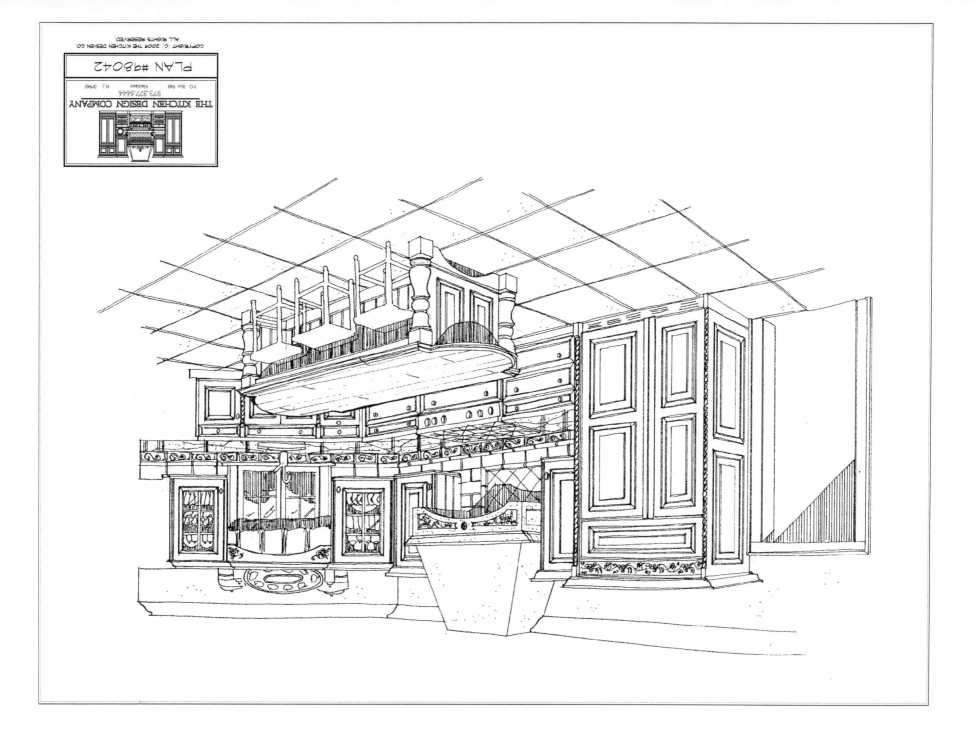

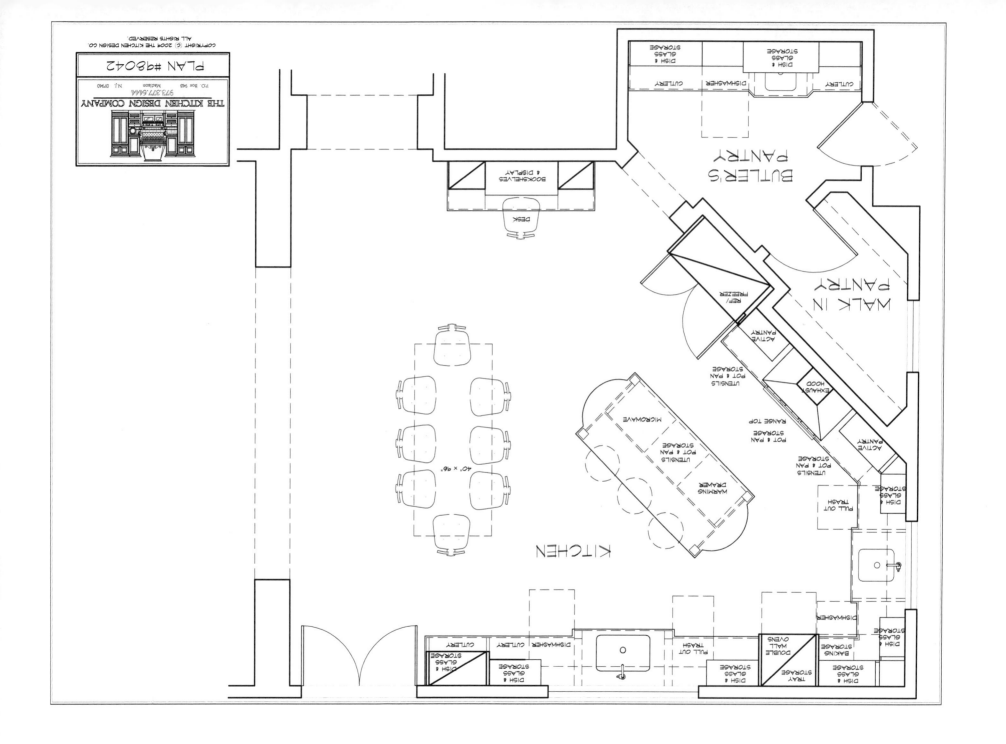

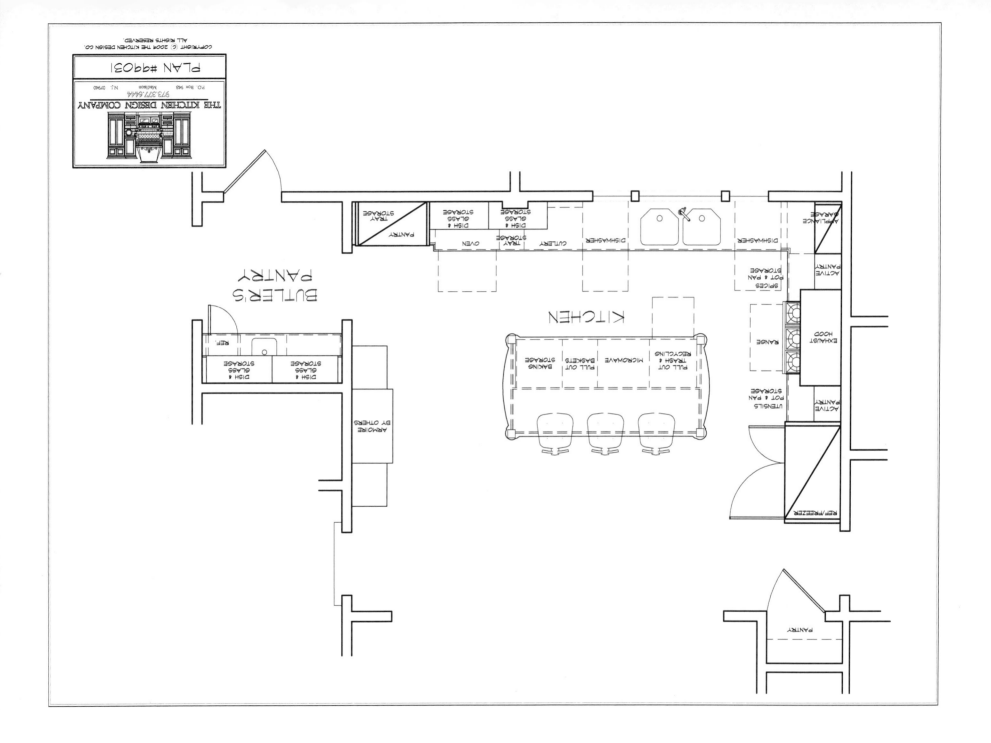

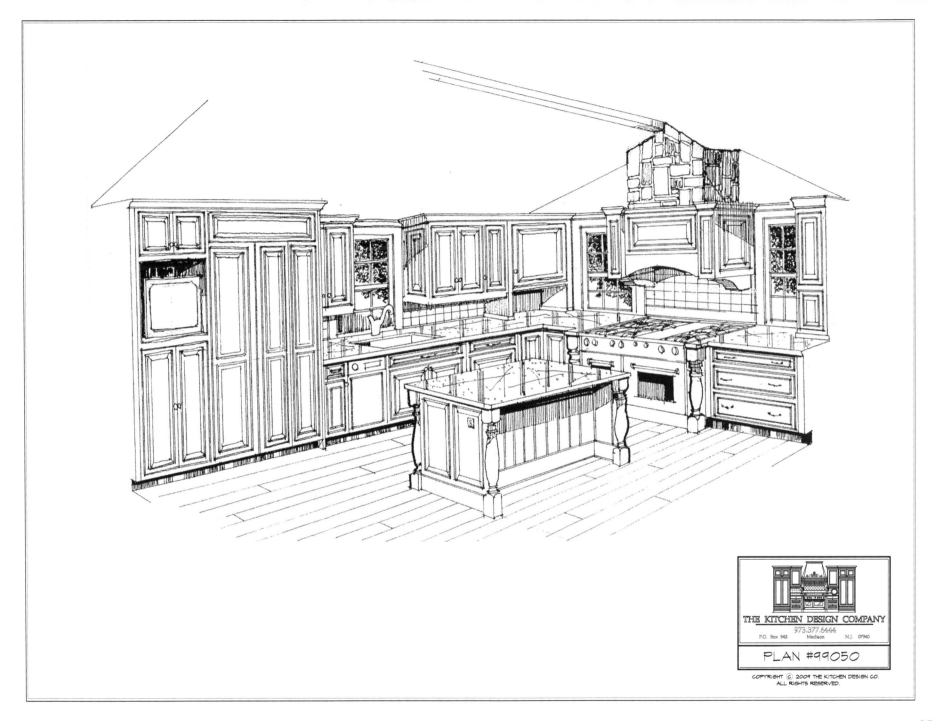

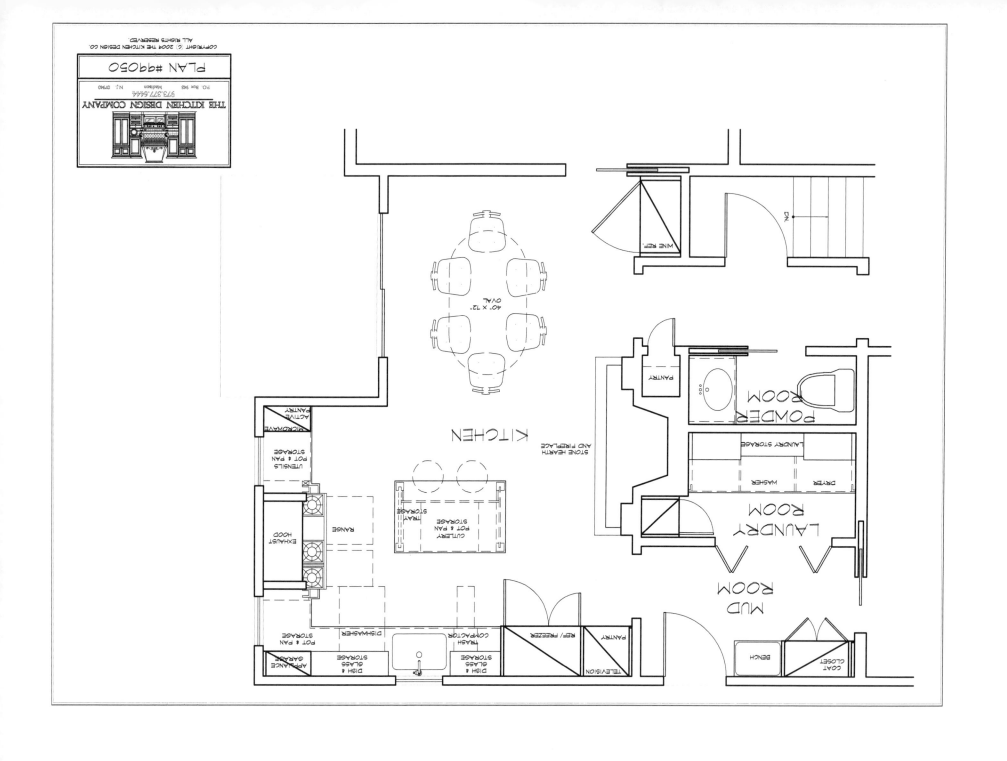

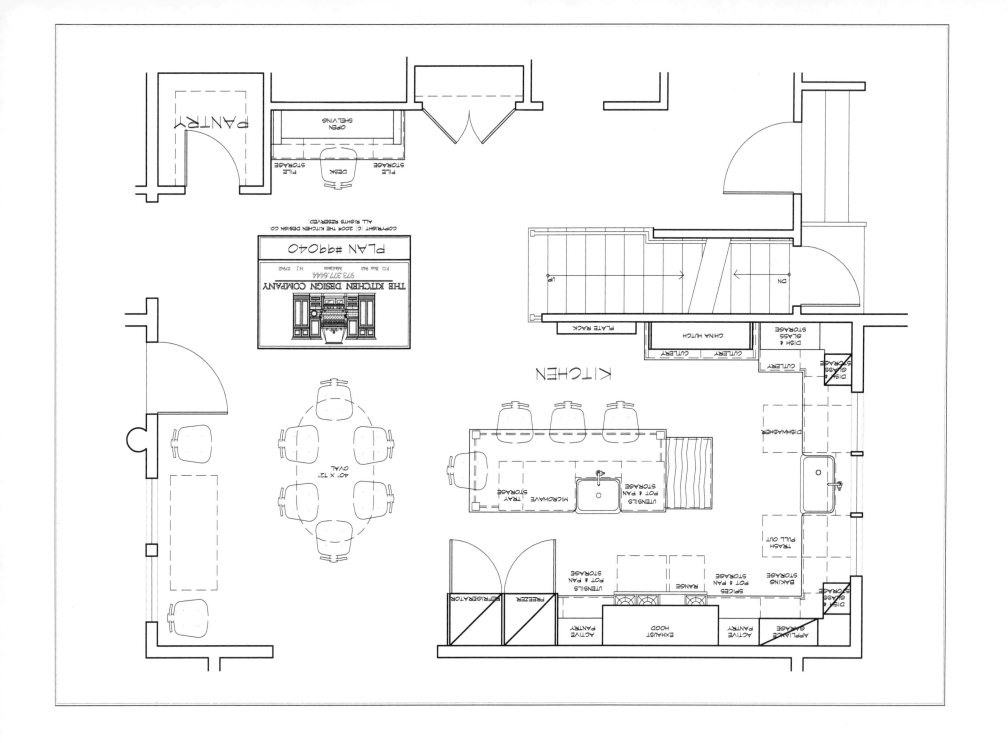

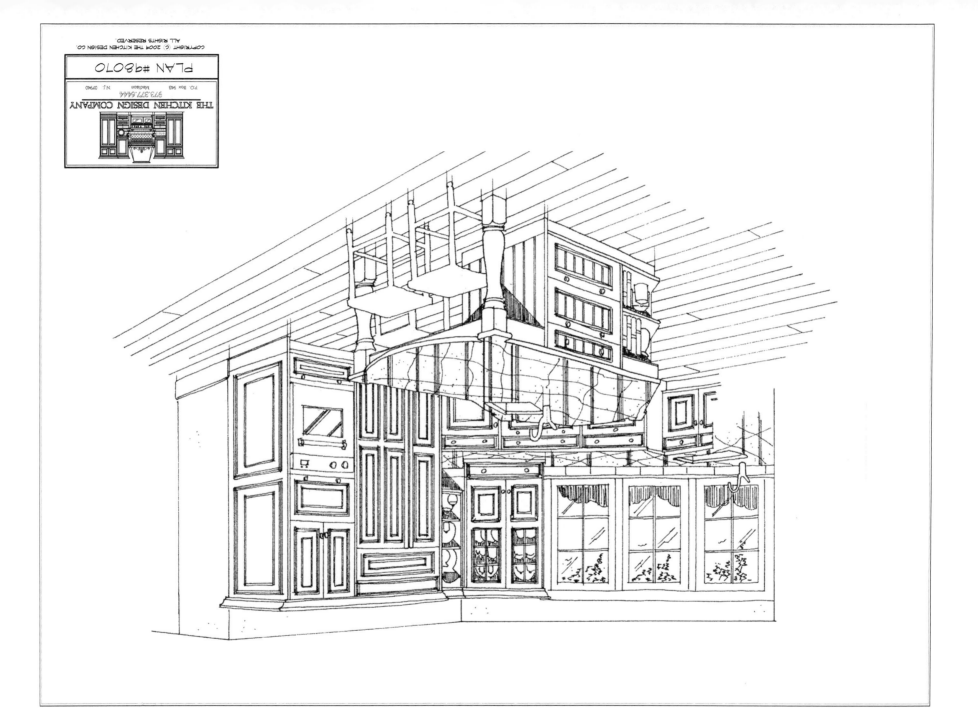

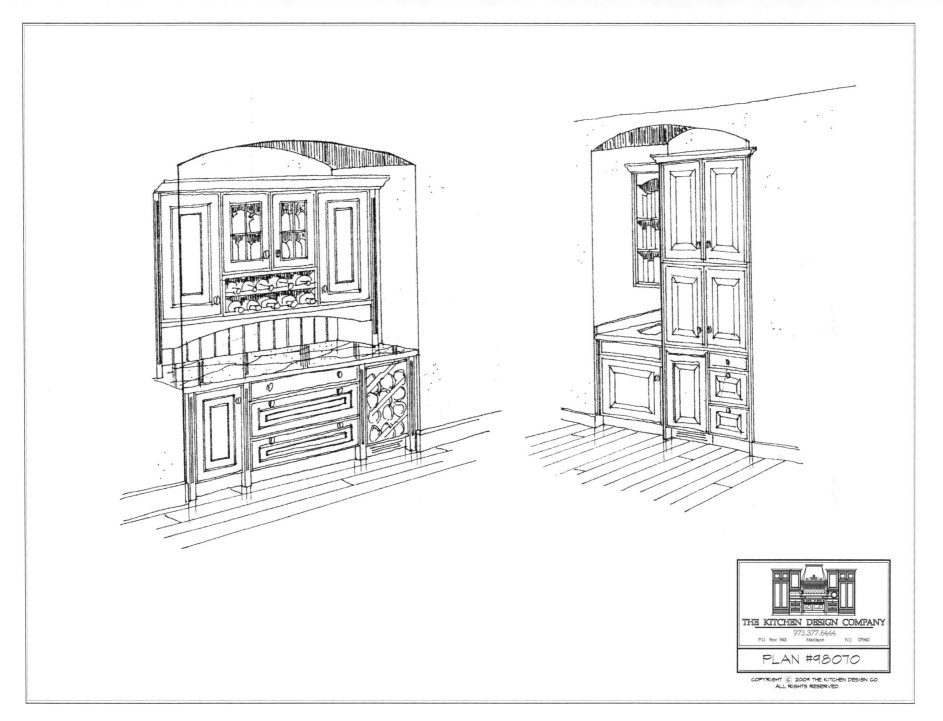

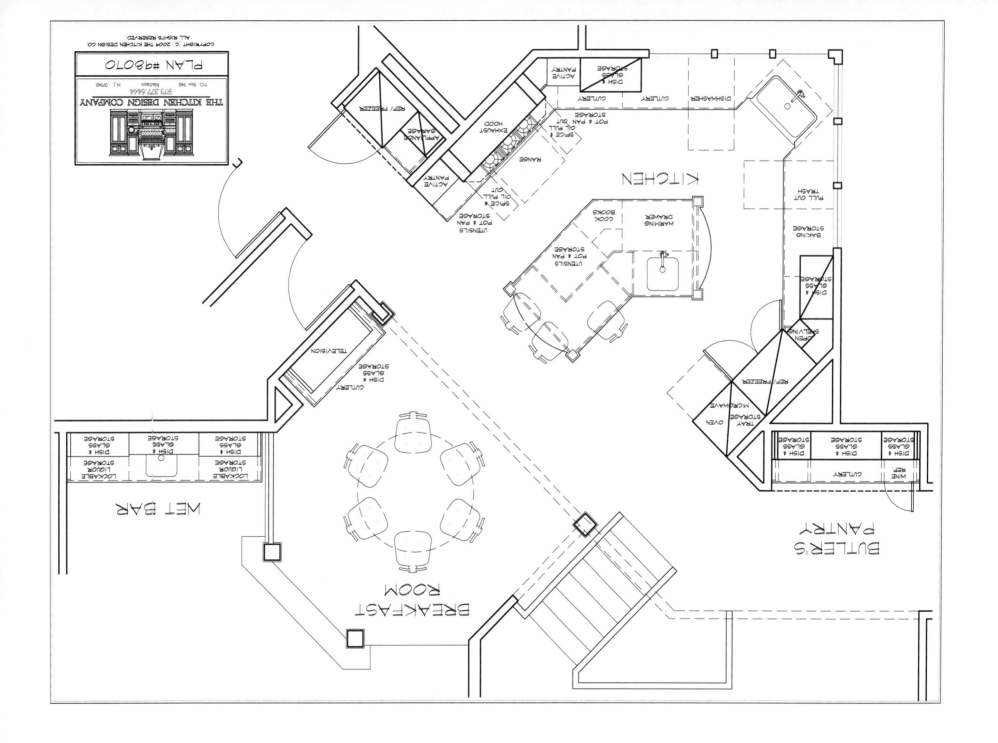

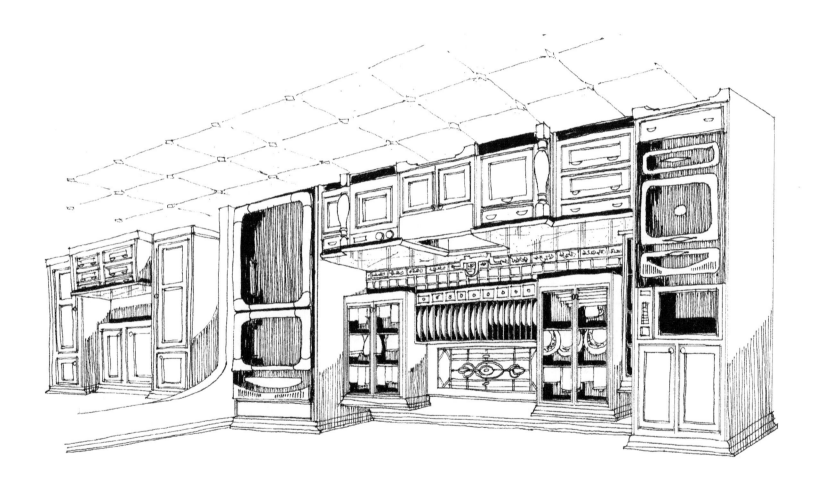

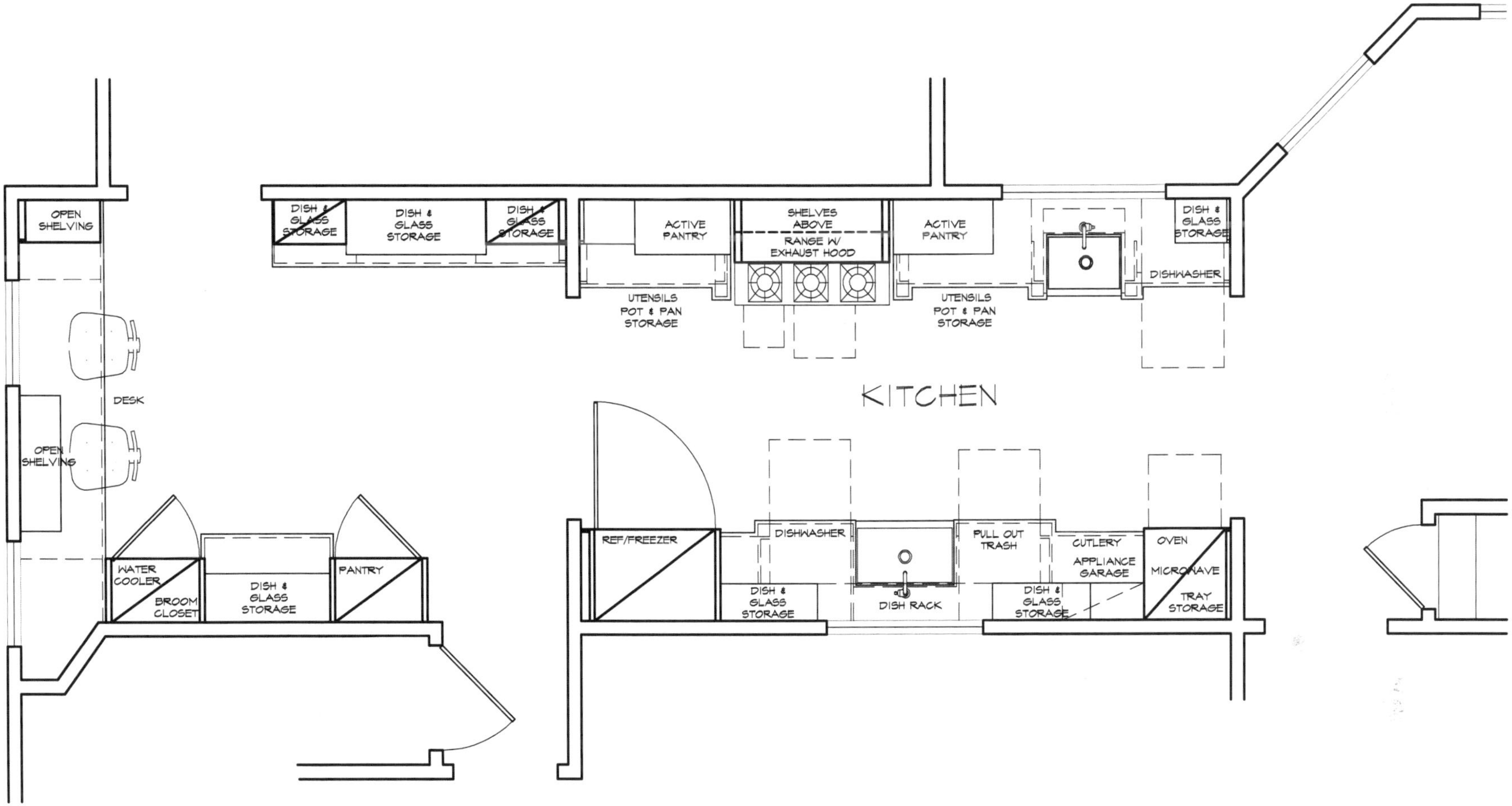

KITCHEN

- OPEN SHELVING
- DISH & GLASS STORAGE
- DISH & GLASS STORAGE
- DISH & GLASS STORAGE
- ACTIVE PANTRY
- SHELVES ABOVE / RANGE W/ EXHAUST HOOD
- ACTIVE PANTRY
- DISH & GLASS STORAGE
- DISHWASHER
- UTENSILS POT & PAN STORAGE
- UTENSILS POT & PAN STORAGE
- DESK
- OPEN SHELVING
- WATER COOLER
- BROOM CLOSET
- DISH & GLASS STORAGE
- PANTRY
- REF/FREEZER
- DISHWASHER
- PULL OUT TRASH
- CUTLERY APPLIANCE GARAGE
- OVEN MICROWAVE
- DISH & GLASS STORAGE
- DISH RACK
- DISH & GLASS STORAGE
- TRAY STORAGE

THE KITCHEN DESIGN COMPANY
973.377.6444
P.O. Box 943 Madison N.J. 07940

PLAN #97038

COPYRIGHT © 2009 THE KITCHEN DESIGN CO.
ALL RIGHTS RESERVED.

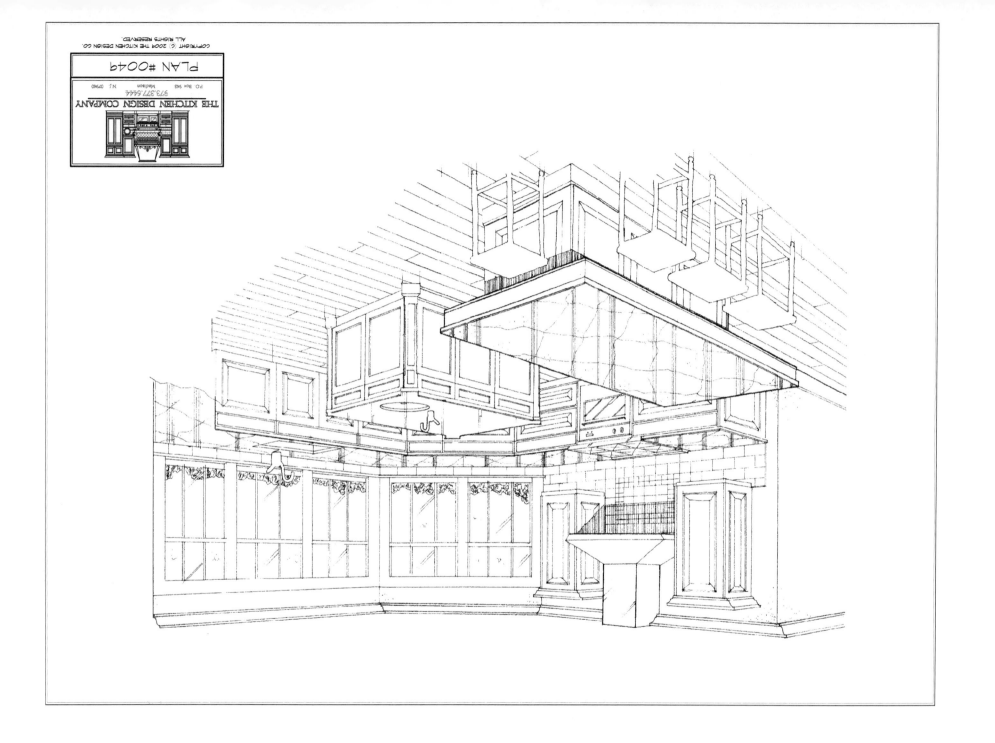

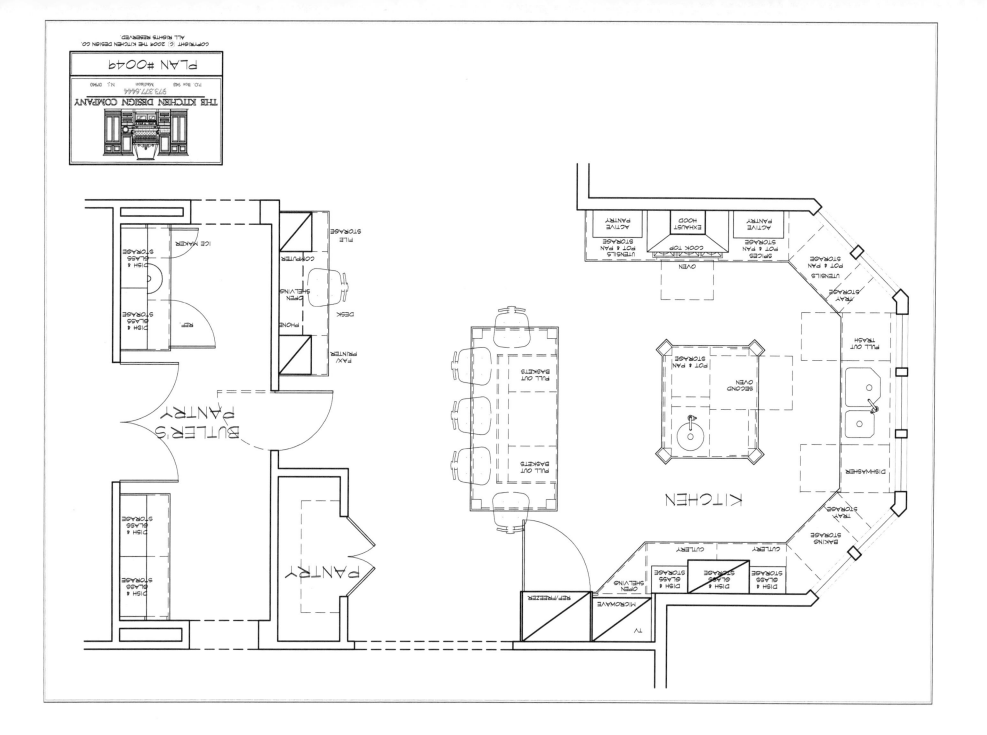

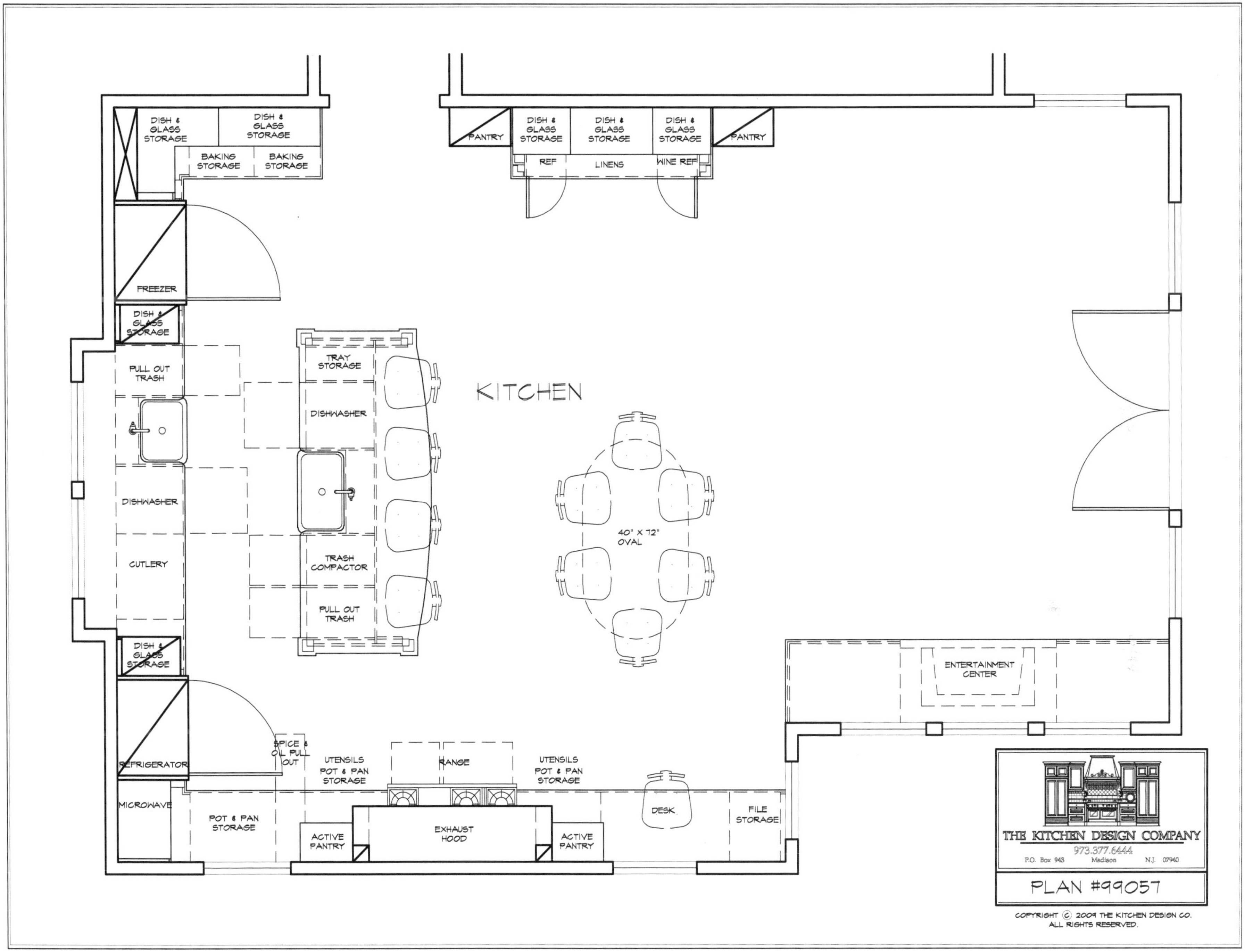
DISH & GLASS STORAGE
DISH & GLASS STORAGE
BAKING STORAGE
BAKING STORAGE
PANTRY
DISH & GLASS STORAGE
DISH & GLASS STORAGE
DISH & GLASS STORAGE
PANTRY
REF
LINENS
WINE REF
FREEZER
DISH & GLASS STORAGE
PULL OUT TRASH
DISHWASHER
CUTLERY
DISH & GLASS STORAGE
REFRIGERATOR
MICROWAVE
TRAY STORAGE
DISHWASHER
TRASH COMPACTOR
PULL OUT TRASH
KITCHEN
40" X 72" OVAL
ENTERTAINMENT CENTER
SPICE & OIL PULL OUT
UTENSILS POT & PAN STORAGE
RANGE
UTENSILS POT & PAN STORAGE
POT & PAN STORAGE
ACTIVE PANTRY
EXHAUST HOOD
ACTIVE PANTRY
DESK
FILE STORAGE
THE KITCHEN DESIGN COMPANY
973.377.6444
P.O. Box 943 Madison N.J. 07940
PLAN #99057
COPYRIGHT © 2009 THE KITCHEN DESIGN CO.
ALL RIGHTS RESERVED.

KITCHEN

MUD ROOM

PLAN #0440

PLAN #0033

THE KITCHEN DESIGN COMPANY
973.377.6444
P.O. Box 943 Madison N.J. 07940

COPYRIGHT (C) 2004 THE KITCHEN DESIGN CO.
ALL RIGHTS RESERVED.

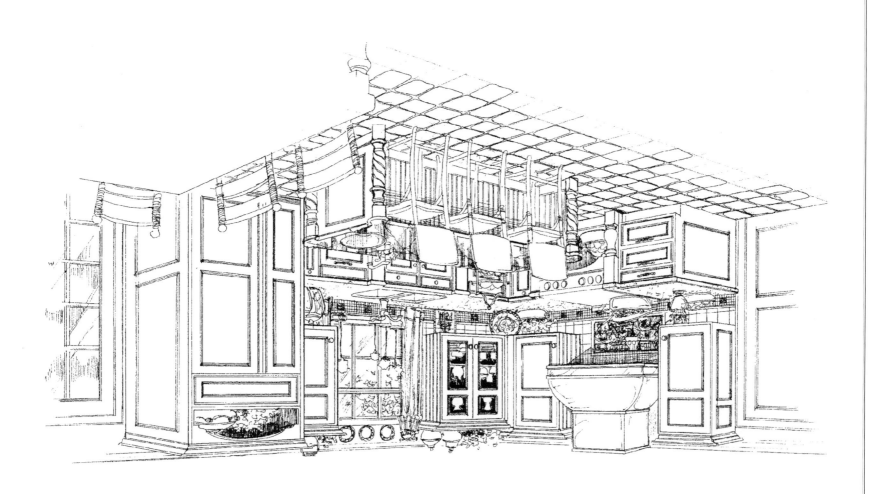

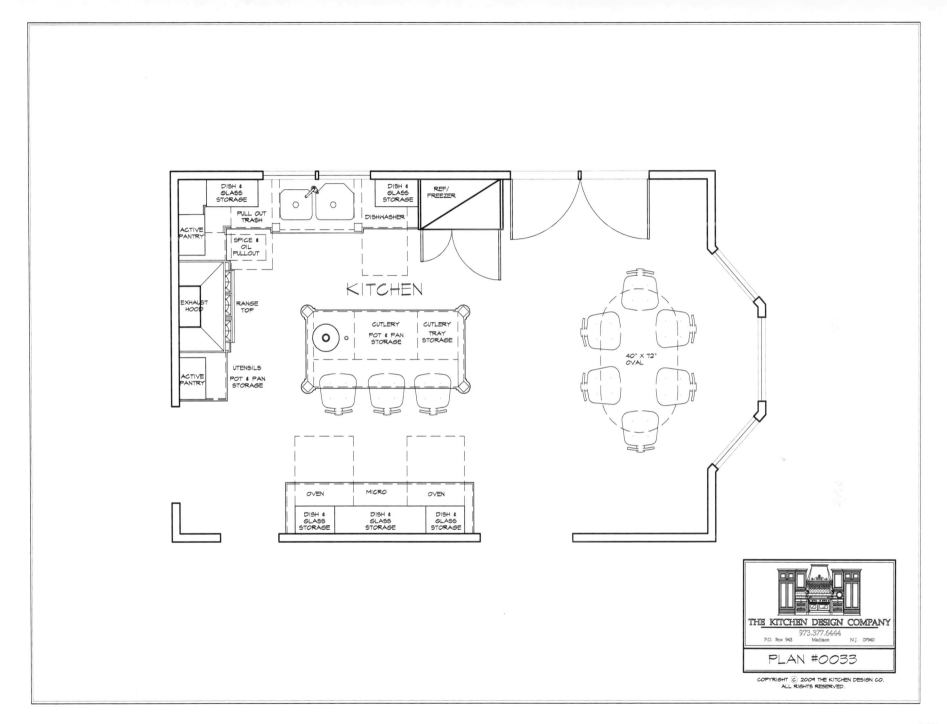

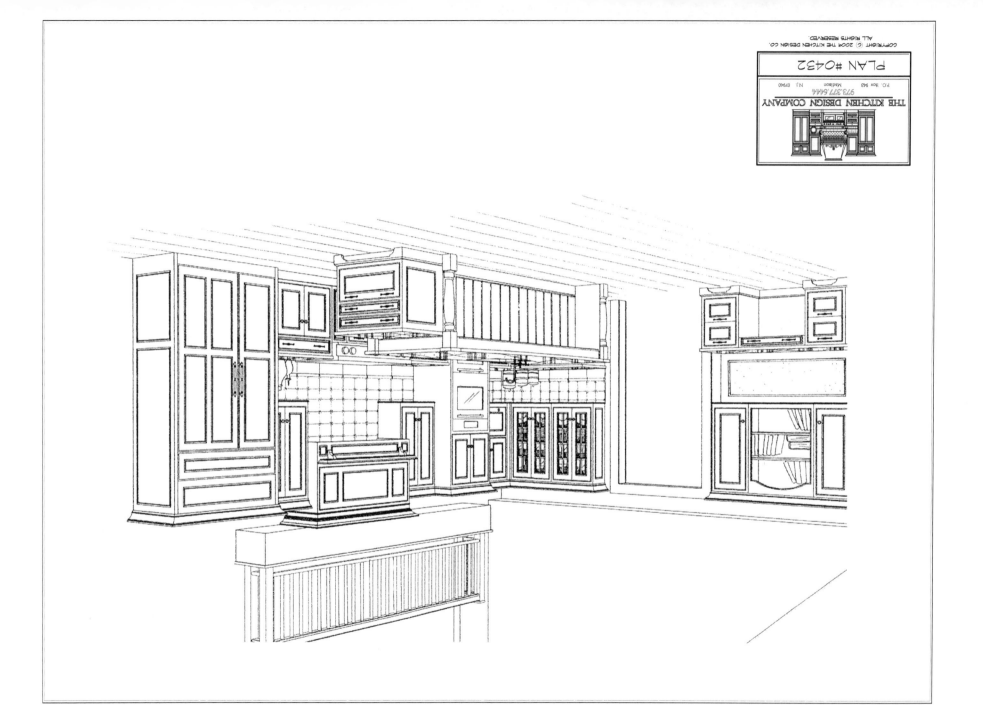

THE KITCHEN DESIGN COMPANY
973.377.6444
P.O. Box 943   Madison   N.J.   07940

PLAN #0432

COPYRIGHT © 2004 THE KITCHEN DESIGN CO.
ALL RIGHTS RESERVED.

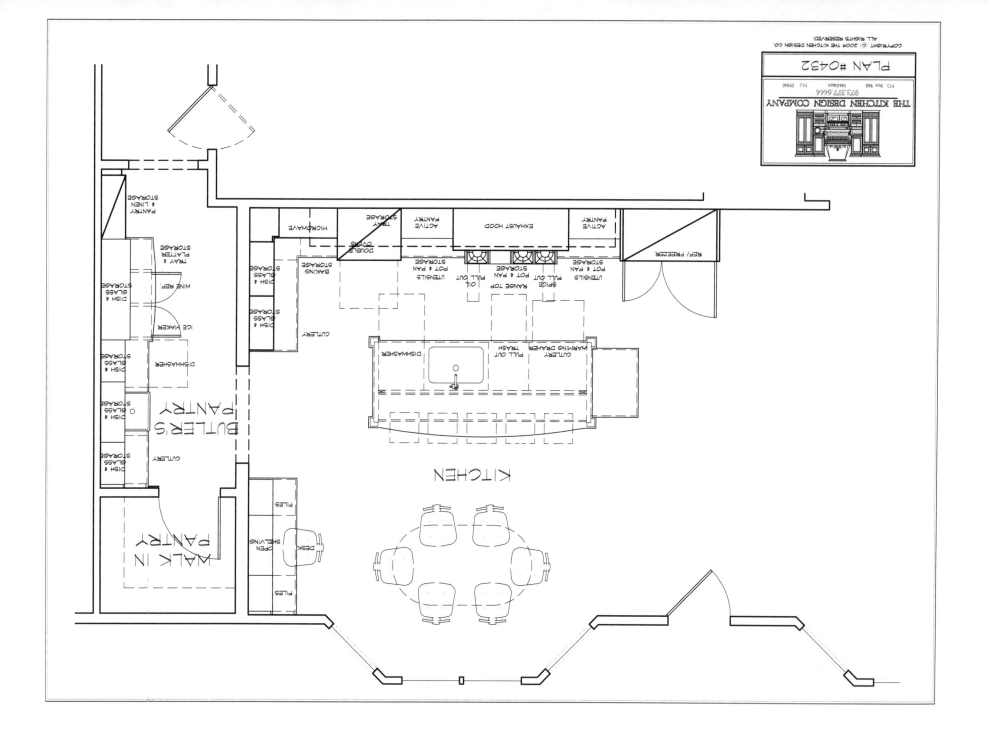

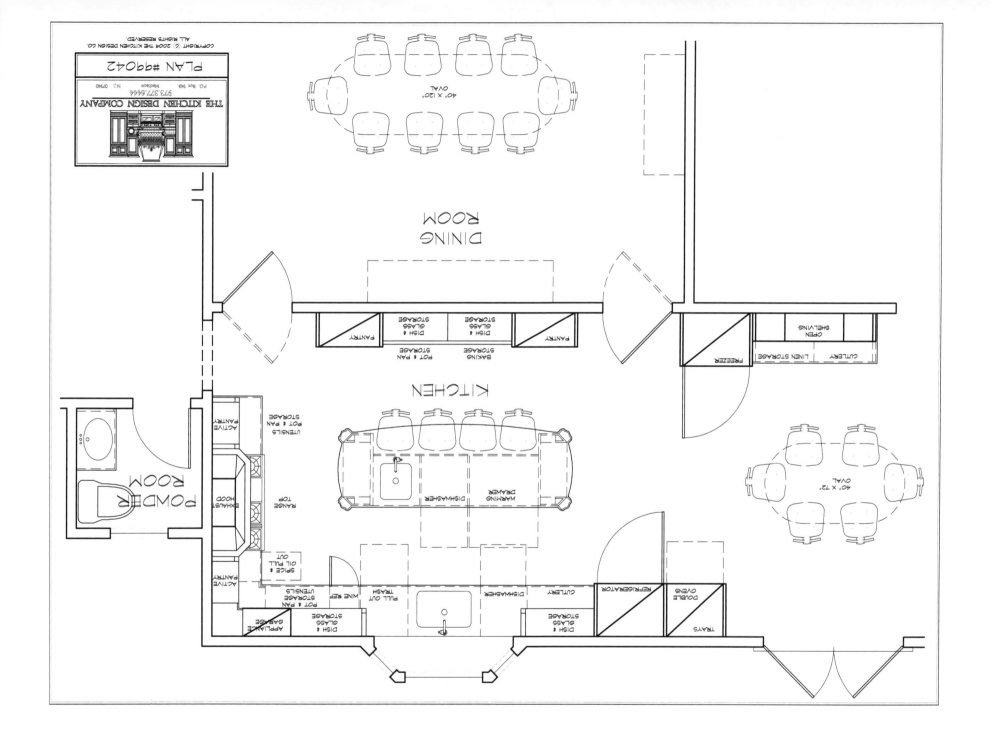

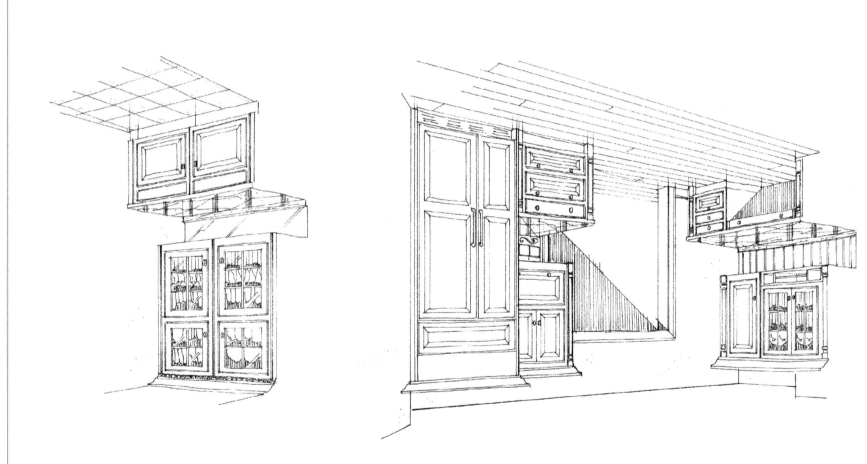

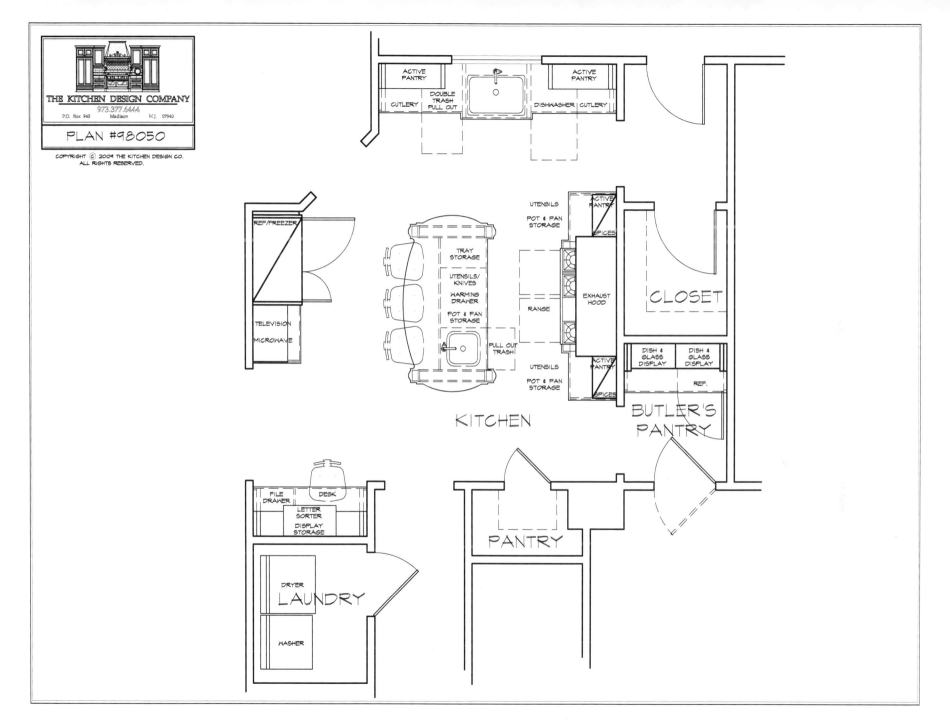

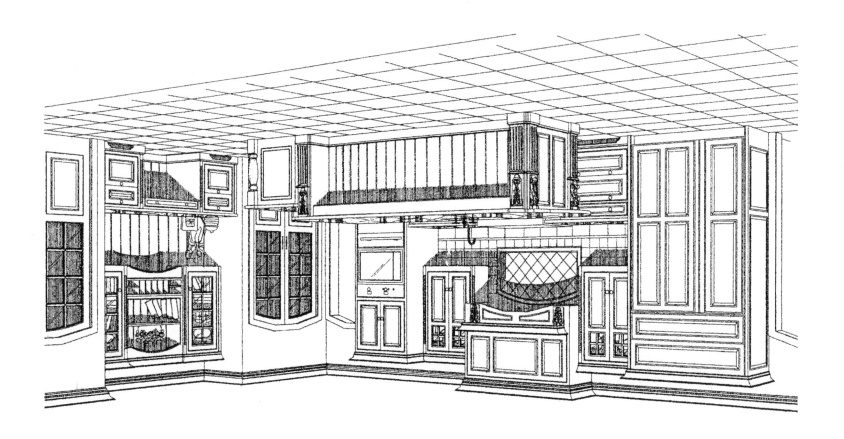

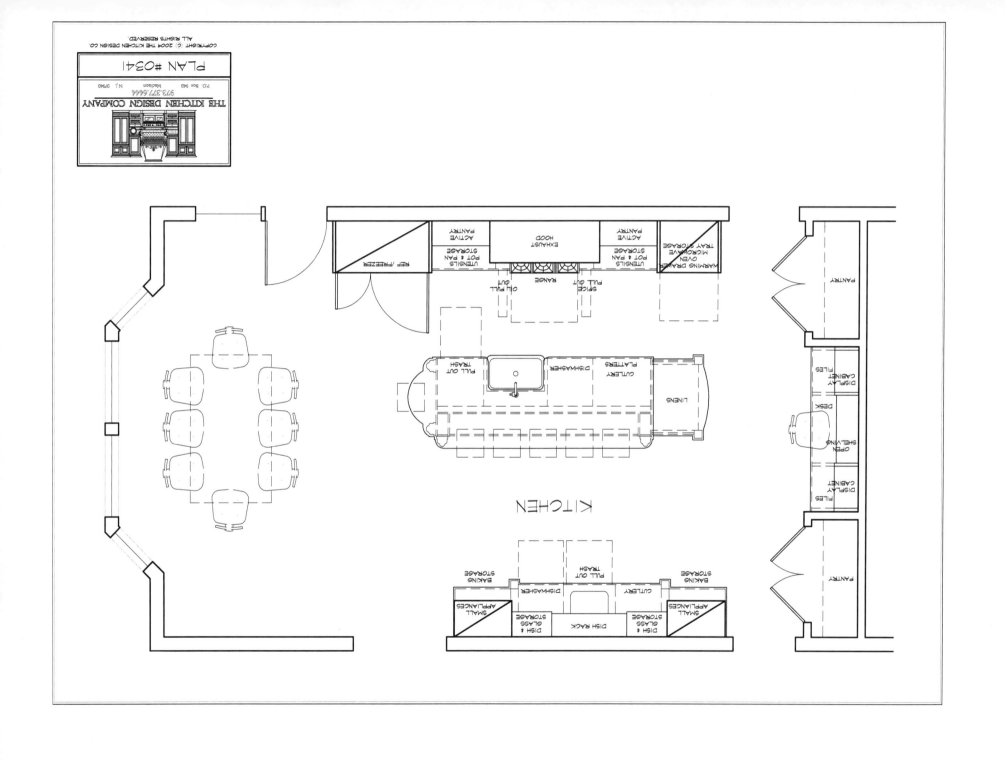

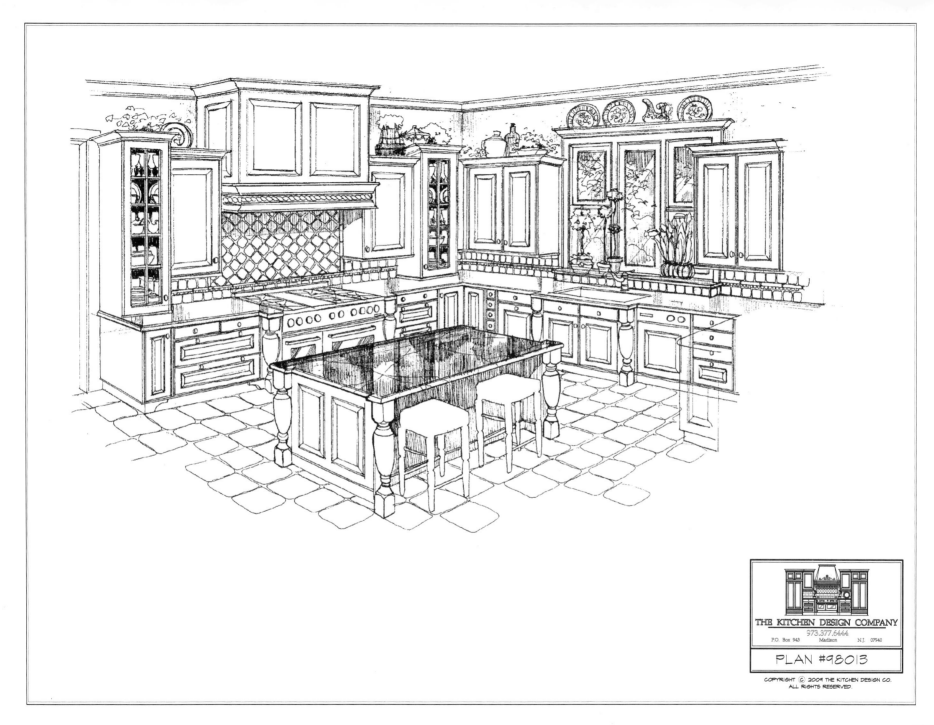

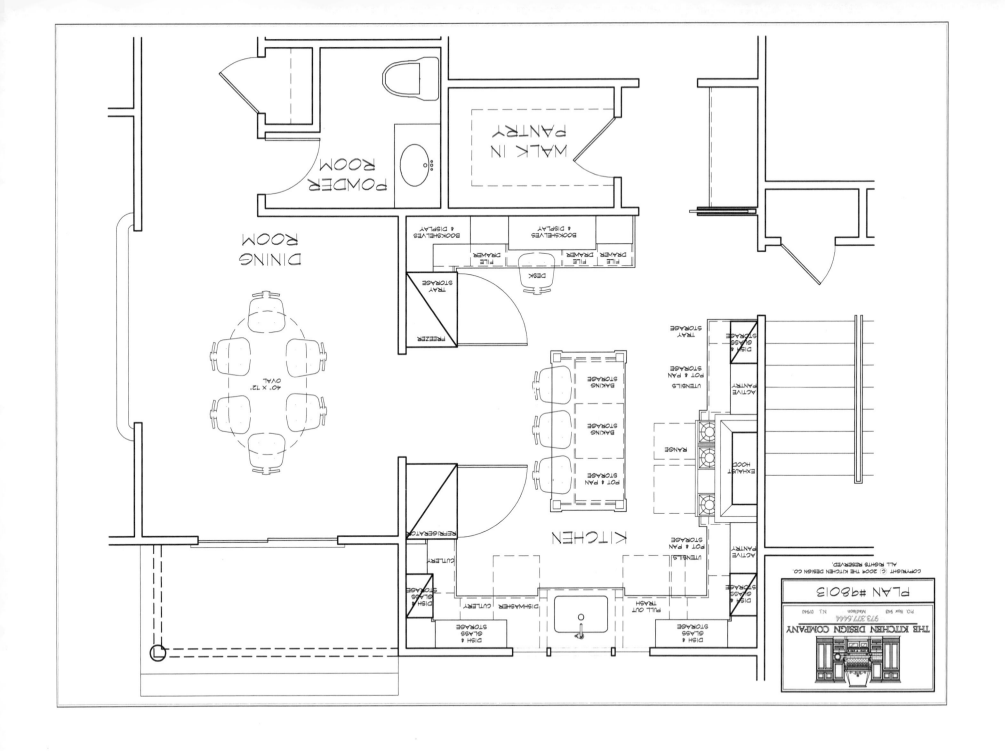

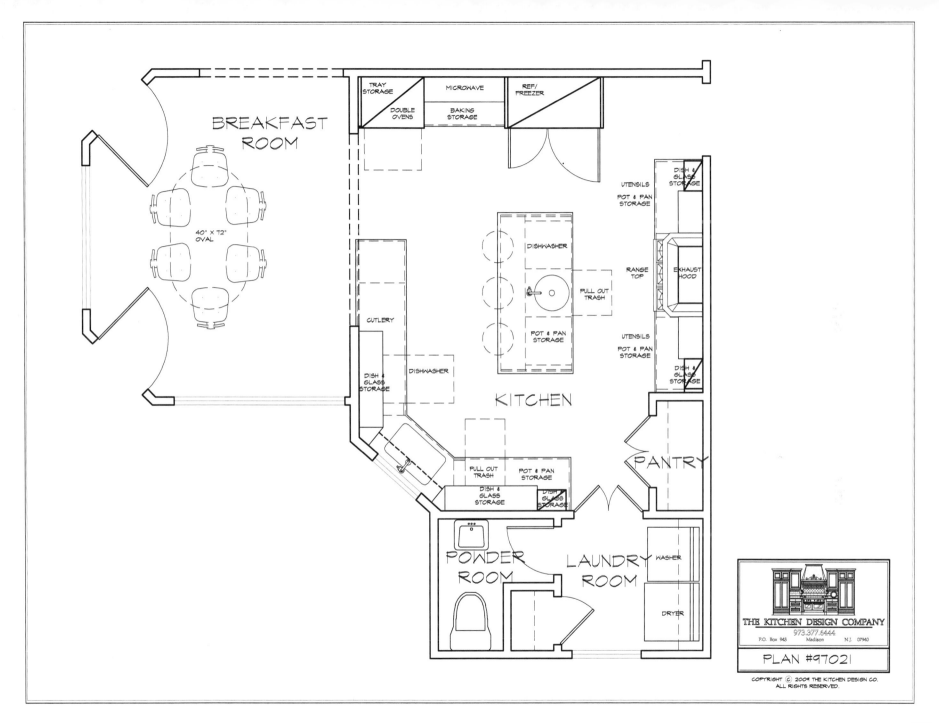

The Kitchen Design Company's

Kitchen Design Book

To Order Any of the Kitchen Drawings in This Idea Book
Go to www.KitchenDesignCo.com/buy-drawings

The Drawings will be sent to you via USPS priority mail. The drawing sheet size is 22" x 17" and drawn at 1/2" = 1'-0" scale.

Shipping and handling cost is fixed at $5.75 us per order for delivery within the United States.

Outside the USA shipping and handling cost is fixed at $26.50 us per order.

You can order:

Individual Drawings
3D Perspectives, or Floor Plans

3D Perspective Drawings Sets
3D Perspectives & Floor Plan of one of the Kitchens

Kitchen Interior Design Drawings (KIDD) Sets
3D Perspectives, Interior Elevations, & Floor Plan of one of the kitchens
(interior elevations & floor plans are dimensioned)

To Order 1 or Multiple copies of Kitchen Perspectives or Kitchen Plans and /or Sets Go to

www.KitchenDesignCo.com/buy-drawings

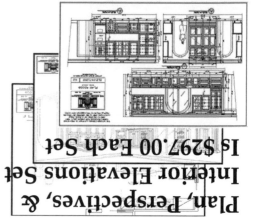

Plan, Perspectives, & Interior Elevations Set is $297.00 Each Set

Plan &Perspectives Drawings Set is $29.97 Each Set

Plan or Perspective Drawings are $9.97 Each Drawing

Printed in Great Britain
by Amazon